NEVER FORGET ANDREW

by

PERRY GROSSER

TELEMACHUS PRESS

Praise for *Never Forget Andrew*

It's impossible as a parent to imagine losing a child and yet it happens every day. Perry Grosser's heart-warming book *Never Forget Andrew* is a reminder that those we love most live on in our hearts and memories. His collection of blog posts, written as a way to remember his son, are a raw look at grief, love, healing and the eternal bond that exists between parent and child. Reading this book will make you hug your loved ones a little tighter and notice the flower in the sidewalk crack.

Lee and Bob Woodruff

This book is a work of non-fiction. The events and characters are true and some names have been changed to protect personal identity.

NEVER FORGET ANDREW

The publisher does not have any control over and does not assume any responsibility for author or third-party websites or their content.

Cover designed by Telemachus Press, LLC

Cover photo and interior photos property of the Perry Grosser Family or reprinted with permission unless noted here:
Copyright © Shutterstock_62738830_Quarter
Copyright © Shutterstock_197808884_Forest Path
Copyright © iStock-512115364_Lucilleb_Park Bench

Published by Telemachus Press, LLC
7652 Sawmill Road
Suite 304
Dublin, Ohio 43016
http://www.telemachuspress.com

Visit the author website:
http://www.NeverForgetAndrew.com

FAM014000 FAMILY & RELATIONSHIPS / Death, Grief, Bereavement

ISBN: 978-1-945330-86-5 (eBook)
ISBN: 978-1-945330-87-2 (Paperback)
ISBN: 978-1-945330-88-9 (Hardback)

Version 2017.12.30
20180117

PREFACE

This book is a compilation of writings about my personal experiences after the sudden loss of our son, Andrew. They are not only stories about Andrew but also about other topics that have resonated with me and my family, friends and many followers on my blog. I write not only for myself, but to be the voice of so many other bereaved parents. I have heard many times over the past few years that I am able to put into words and paragraphs what others are feeling and thinking, but unable to write. My writing, as well as this book, have become the voice of many bereaved parents. What I have experienced and written about is not unique to me—but is common to many bereaved parents.

This book is intended to be a resource to help bereaved parents and those who care for them, to understand and deal with the loss of their children. I know that these parents will never be whole again, and the pain will last a lifetime, but I do hope some aspect of the book resonates with you and not only brings some comfort and peace but also lets you know that you are not alone in your grief…

Please share some of your own personal experiences by posting comments on our website:

www.NeverForgetAndrew.com

Thank you,

Perry Grosser
December 2017

ACKNOWLEDGEMENTS

My son Andrew is my inspiration for writing this book. During his lifetime, I learned a great deal from Andrew and I continue to learn through him, especially now. Living with his loss, as difficult as it is, I wrote this book. As a parent, my responsibility is to do everything in my power to protect my children. I can no longer do this for Andrew, so writing this book is my way of keeping some part of him alive. As Andrew's father, it is my obligation and honor to keep his name and his legacy alive.

I want to thank my editors, Susan Cullen Wallace, Andrew Samett, and Sharon Lerner. They read and edited every chapter. They read through my raw emotions and tears to edit my words into chapters that others can read and benefit from. Through their feedback and edits, I have become a better writer. I am forever thankful for the time and effort they provided over the past few years. Each of them knew Andrew, so they could hear his voice through my words and see the smile on his face that I talk about.

Thank you to the readers and subscribers of my website, especially to those who took the time to respond with hundreds of comments and e-mails. Seeing the thousands of page views the days following my posts helped to sustain me and keep me going.

I want to thank Steven Himes and MaryAnn Nocco of Telemachus Press. They helped me navigate this entire publishing project and were there to answer my questions and point me in the right direction at all times.

My lovely wife of thirty years, Dorothy: Thank you. She has always been behind me nudging me along with her unrelenting support, in front of me setting a path to follow, and beside me holding my hand. We have cried together, we have smiled together, and we are on this path together for Andrew. Thank you.

Nicole, my amazing daughter, is the light in my eye, the reason I get up every morning, and the deepest motivation of my life. She is brilliant (which she gets from her mom), has a wonderfully contagious laugh (which she gets from my sister, Laurie), and amazing compassion (which she gets from both her Grandmas). She has the entire world before her now and I want to stick around to see what she does with it.

Finally, thank you, my nephews Todd and Greg, for calling me and checking in on your uncle on a regular basis. Your thoughtfulness and telephone calls over the past four years have helped to keep my heart strong.

TABLE OF CONTENTS

NEVER FORGET ANDREW

HELLO
January 29, 2014

I HAVE SET up Andrew's site. I don't want to call it a memorial site, or a blog. It is going to be an ongoing project about Andrew's life and our memories of my son, as well as other people's memories about him.

I find great comfort in writing about Andrew. I can't say I enjoy it, because I am not sure what I enjoy in my life anymore without him, but I find it very helpful to write about him. Some of the posts will be sad, about our missing him. Others will be more upbeat about the good times we had and the positive effects Andrew had on so many lives. I have never written for my friends or the public at large, so please bear with me as I learn this process.

Of my daughter Nicole: She has always been the light in my life alongside her brother, she is what keeps me going, she is where I have always found joy and happiness, and even more so now. If it were not for her I am not sure where I would be now or headed in the future. But in her, I have a continued purpose in life, and my life has meaning. And for that I am forever grateful.

I have written one post which I am going to edit and post sometime soon. Any feedback, comments, anything, is greatly appreciated. If you read something that stirs you, that affects you or your life, or that brings a smile to your face, or tears, I would appreciate it if you could write a comment on the post. That way I know that people are reading it, and that there is purpose in what I am doing, beyond that of finding peace within myself and my life.

Thank you,
Perry
Andrew's Dad

CONGRATULATIONS, ANDREW

February 1, 2014

CONGRATULATIONS.

This is hardly a way to start a post on a site focused on my grieving for my son, but with this one it is appropriate.

A couple of months after Andrew passed, my wife Dorothy and I received a nondescript padded 11" x 14" envelope in the mail from the University of Colorado at Boulder, Andrew's school. We opened it and to our surprise it was Andrew's college diploma from CU Boulder. The school graduated Andrew and sent us his diploma. We cried all night--but tears of happiness, for a change. For three years Andrew worked very hard for this diploma. He studied in the library at night, he studied over the weekends, he wrote papers, and took a lot of tests. This is the first thing in Andrew's life that he really, really worked hard for, that he saw value in, and he knew that he was working hard for it. And in these last three years it changed him for the better.

Those who knew Andrew knew that, through no fault of his own, he had a way of not having to work hard. He practiced very hard in hockey and worked hard during the games, but he loved that and enjoyed it, so it was not really hard work for him. High school was rather easy for him. He did not do much studying or homework and did not have to work very hard during the day, at school, and still he got A's and B's. He learned to snowboard in a matter of a couple of hours, and, when he forgot his boots one day, he rented a pair of skis and spent all day skiing like a pro. He picked up on driving very quickly, and after only a few months took his road test and scored a perfect score with absolutely no points taken off. Yes, I am sure there were things that challenged him in his short life, but he had never before really worked as hard as he had to work to earn his college degree.

We learned that it was his fellow psychology students, teachers, and professors who requested that the school graduate him and issue him his diploma. That was so amazingly kind and compassionate of so

many people. He was only two core courses away from graduation, and I am sure that this little piece of paper with some words and his name scrolled on it means so much to him.

It brought back memories of when Andrew graduated from high school. He had a huge smile across his face, he felt so accomplished he was headed to Colorado, his whole life ahead of him. He was so happy. He was typical Andrew—he wore his sandals and had his Aber

crombie shorts and a T-shirt on under his unzipped gown.

We are going to be happy when all of his friends and his two cousins graduate from college this May. We know that Andrew would be proud of them all. We are just going to be sad that he won't be walking

down the aisle by himself or with them, but he will be looking over them from above.

We have the diploma in the padded folding case that it came in on a table in the living room along with his pictures and other treasures of his life. We look at it every day and we are so proud of him that he got so far.

WHAT CAN I SAY? THERE ARE NO WORDS

February 3, 2014

A VERY CLOSE friend of mine's elderly father is very close to the end of his time. Maybe days, maybe weeks or months. He has been in and out of the hospital and hospice, and every time someone sees him, it might be their last. But that is not the point of this post. I talk to my friend and I am at a loss as to what I can say about what he is going through. The words just are not there.

My father passed away when I was young, sixteen, suddenly, without warning, and while he was away from home. I talk to my friend and I listen to what he is going through, and although I listen and understand and feel for him, I just cannot emotionally relate to it and cannot empathize with him. I don't have the mutual experience and have never gone through the pain and agony of a parent slowly drawn to death. I know, or think I know, that it is very difficult, emotionally draining, and almost all-consuming of life. But I have no reference point to truly empathize with him, although as his friend I can sympathize with him. I never went through it, I never had the experience of those emotions. Although we talk, and I listen to him, and I give him words of encouragement and try to ease his pain, I am at a loss to really know what to say. It is a horrible feeling to be with someone and not be able to ease their pain.

What is the point of this you ask? Well, almost all of you, my friends, relatives, and colleagues, are in the same situation I am in. But with Dorothy and me, you want to help, you want to comfort us, you want to help us heal, but you don't know what to say. You are at a loss for words. You look at us and the words just fail to come out. We cannot count how many times people look at us and have said that they feel bad because they don't know what to say. Some people have actually avoided us because they are at a loss for words, or they can't deal with our loss. Trust me, what happened to us is not contagious.

We understand. We really do. We are thankful that you are blessed and do not share our pain, that you have not experienced the devastating loss that we have and which we live with each and every day, that you go home at night and kiss your children good-night. We are truly happy for you.

What I know is that anything that you say to us or do with us helps. Sometimes it is not words. Sometimes just a hug means so much to us. Yeah, we might cry, but we need to. And if you cry with us, that is fine as well. Andrew touched so many lives that people have to cry to remember and grieve him. A short e-mail or letter saying that you are thinking about us makes all the difference in our day. We thank those of you who have spent time with us to talk about life, make us smile, make us laugh a bit, and bring some joy to our lives. We are happy to get a letter in the mail telling us you are thinking about us, or sharing with us a story about Andrew that we have never heard. A hug. A hello. Something to read about him, or tell us what is going on in your life—everything helps.

What can I say? There are no words. There are no words that will make us feel better. There are no words that will bring our son home. There are no words that will make us stop our grieving. So don't feel bad when you cannot find the words to say to us when you see us or talk to us. There are no words.
There are no words.

MY FATHER AND MY SON
February 8, 2014

I DID SOMETHING that was so hard for me to do a couple of weeks ago. I said Kaddish for both my father and my son, together. It has been hard to say it for my dad for the past thirty-four years. Every time I say it I try to recall him, try to remember the times we had together. Every year it gets harder and harder as I get older and the memories of when I was a boy fade with age. It has been devastatingly  hard to say Kaddish for Andrew since September. I cry every single time I stand, thinking about him and how much I miss my son.

 But saying it together for them made me think about them more than cry over them. It was a very introspective experience.

What goes on in Heaven? My father was there for thirty-four years before Andrew was called.

Was my father there to meet and welcome his grandson and

make the transition easier for him? Nicole asked that the Angels lead Andrew into heaven. Was my dad one of those angels? Andrew does not know many people in heaven. Of course, he knew Dorothy's father (and I am sure he is holding him), and Aunt Flo and Uncle Cy, who loved him dearly. But he has no friends or close relatives that went before him to help him. I know that he felt lost and alone and dealt with anxiety sometimes here on earth, not sure where to go, what to do, or whom to hold. I hope that did not follow him and that his pain was left here on earth.

What I picture in my mind over and over again is Andrew and Dad sitting at a wood picnic bench high in the mountains talking to each other and sharing stories about me. They both loved the mountains and this image brings me great peace.

My father knew me for only 16 years, 2 months, 10 days, or 5915 days. That was way too short to really get to know me, and I know that I really never got to know my father the way a son should. But we had great times. We went cross-country as a family twice, we went on many, many wonderful vacations, and we learned to SCUBA dive together and dove together for a few years. He helped me in school, and helped me through my youth riddled with ADD, OCD, and hyper-activity, and he was always there to help me. But sixteen years was way too short to really understand me as a person, and for me to really appreciate how much I needed him throughout my life. All of his memories of me were as a boy, and just into my teen years.

My own son, Andrew, did not fare much better, he knew me for 21 years, 7 months, 27 days, or 7910 days. He knew me as his father, as his protector, and as someone he could always count on. We also went on many great vacations, some cruises, and he, too, got SCUBA-certified and we went on many dives along with Nicole and Dorothy. Each and every dive was a great experience. Andrew and I talked for hours on end about life, about what he wanted to do when he graduated, and about everything from the Beatles to computers. I, too, helped my son through a myriad of issues with his ADD, ADHD, stress, and his kidney stones. It was always a challenge and it made me appreciate what my mom and dad went through with me growing up. It was a challenge, but I know that he knew I always had his back and that I always was there to support, protect, and defend him.

So now I sit here alone at my table, thinking about them, knowing that my son and my father are together talking about me. They are sharing stories, laughing, holding hands and smiling, thankful for the time each of them had with me here on earth, knowing that they both loved me, and knowing that I loved them both so much and miss them both so much. They never met in life, but they are now forever together for eternity in heaven. This picture in my mind brings me so much peace.

Maybe, one day, many years down the road, I will join them at that park bench and set the stories straight.

CAN WE HAVE A GOOD TIME?
February 14, 2014

DOROTHY AND I went out the other day. It was the first time we actually went to "something" other than go out to dinner with a few friends. And it was nice. We had a good time, all things considered.

We were invited to a wine auction luncheon for the Rockland Center for the Arts by one of my closest friends' mother, someone whom I have been calling Mom for over forty years. It took us a couple of weeks of introspection to accept Molly's invitation, but she was very happy we did. We had to really think about it. Was it too soon? Would we feel guilty going out and having a good time? There would be no one there other than Molly, my friend and his fiancée, and another couple, whom she invited, who knew us and who could come over and say they were sorry. We would have our own car, so if we needed to we could leave at any time. We knew the restaurant and the owner, so we felt like it would be a safe place for us. It actually is one of Andrew's favorite eateries—X2O in Yonkers. When we told Molly we would go, she was very happy, and we felt a certain sense of relief, as well as other feelings we really cannot explain.

Does this mean we are "better"? Are we finally "over it"? Absolutely not. Not on your life. This means that we realize that we still have to live and continue on with our lives, which we always knew, but could not accept. This means that we can get out of the house and be with others, that we could have a nice time with others, and yet still think and talk about Andrew. Which we did at lunch. We told stories about him, we remembered him, knowing we all love and miss him so very much. We talked about when we grew up, we talked about our dads, and we talked about their upcoming wedding. We talked a lot. What was important was that we were able to go out, be with friends, enjoy ourselves, and still grieve for our son. And we could be with others who understood this. This is a big step. We are forever grateful for the invitation, Molly,

Will we be over it soon, or ever? No. We will never be over it, we can't be. But we can live our lives, our new lives, to some degree. We are always one question, or one story, or seeing one person, away from being in tears. As I have said before, we are different people now, we are not the same people we were five months ago. There are people who want us to be who we were, they want the old Perry and Dorothy and Nicole back. That won't happen. But our friends and relatives are ready to accept who we are now. And that is so much appreciated. If you're waiting for us to be our old selves, or waiting for us to be over our loss and our grief, we are sorry to say that that will never be. Actually, we are not sorry. We want to, and need to, be new people. People who remember our son, who can talk about him and accept us as we are now is what we ask for. It might be a hard concept for some people to accept, but we ask that you do.

We are still not ready to go out to a party. We are still not ready to laugh and be part of a large gathering, but we are getting there. Bear with us.

By the way, we did bid on and win a very special bottle of wine at the auction. Now we cherish this bottle and await the perfect time to open it and share it with friends.

A TRUE INSIGHT INTO ANDREW— HIS BUCKET LIST
February 17, 2014

WHILE CLEANING UP Andrew's room a while ago (that is

a post all by itself one day), I came across a few file folders on his shelf. There were no papers or anything in them so I was about to throw them out when I looked inside one of them and what I found amazed me. I found Andrew's Bucket List. I sat down on the edge of his bed and read what I had found over and over again. It is truly an entry into my son's personality, into his mind, into his amazing sense of humor, and into his true compassion as a human being. I showed it to his friend Wally, who said he remembered seeing it a few years ago and thinks Andrew wrote it while a junior in high school. Not a project or an assignment—just something that he wanted to have.

Below is what he had on his list, the list of what he wanted to accomplish in his life before he left this world. Most people make this list later on in life, when it is usually too late to fulfill the list. With Andrew everything had to be done early, so he did it at eighteen or nineteen. While he was able to accomplish only a few of his dreams, what he listed is truly insightful. Read it slowly, and think about each one. You will come away from this list a changed person, I promise.

Bucket List

Get out of Harrison alive

Visit Amsterdam / Europe / Australia

Own a pet monkey

See someone hit by a car and have his shoes come off

Skydive

Own a pool full of Jello or pudding

Live in Colorado at some point of my life

Save 1 life

Live on an island (but not the island from Lost, it confuses me too much)

Count cards in Vegas

Meet a Ninja

Become a Ninja

Learn to surf

Read a book all the way through

Write/Publish a book

Have a water fountain in my house that is filled with fruit punch

Lucid dream

Don't get kicked out of college (for not going to class)

Citizen arrest a cop
Parachute from a plane onto a mountain and snowboard down
Blow up something with my mind
Take a vow of silence
Cure cancer
Never fail a class
Go back in time and stop the following from happening:
Movies: The Happening
The caveman in the GEICO commercial gets his own show
Ms. Fitzsimons from being allowed to coach.

There are so many things I can write about on this list, I can go into each one and it would take weeks of journals, and eventually I might. But there are a few I want to highlight that really touched me.

The first one, and it was probably the most important item to him, and the deepest, is "Save 1 life." In his passing, I think he did accomplish this one item. Actually, I think he may have saved several lives in his passing. His friends told me that they cannot believe he is gone. Of all the kids they knew, all those who lived on the edge, all those who experimented with drugs, drove recklessly, played with knives, pushed the limits as hard as they could, Andrew was none of these. He was the safe one, he was the cautious one. Yes, he drove fast, and smoked a little weed years ago, but he was the funny one, he was the smart one, he was the last one whom death would come after. And yet he is gone the first. This scared a lot of his friends, and maybe, just maybe, saved a life or two—I would like to think so.

Cure cancer. What 17-year-old thinks of that? But his compassion for others, and his want to help others made him put that on his list. I am not sure he really thought he could do this, but he did dream.

He did Get out of Harrison alive, and he did Live in Colorado. He was so thrilled to be out there, he loved the mountains, he loved to snowboard, and he was away from the politics and the crap that runs this town. He took a lot of pictures of Colorado, they are on his iPhone and on his laptops, so that if and when he came back here, he could always look at them and remember how beautiful it was and how much he loved living there.

But he also took some very nice pictures around the house here in Harrison, and the people here, so that if he did not get back he would have them to look at. I will post those pictures sometime soon, they are really nice.

Own a pet monkey? Become a Ninja? Citizen arrest a cop? Blow up something with my mind? He was a funny little boy and it does show. I am sure he would have owned the monkey and arrested the cop if the situation presented itself.

He never Failed a class, and he never Got kicked out of college. He graduated from college and that would have made him happy, although not on his list.

There are some things I never knew he wanted to do. Skydive. Parachute from an airplane and snowboard down a mountain. Lucid dream. Visit Amsterdam/Europe/Australia. If only I had known these things I would have done what I could to make them happen. We had time when he was home and if I had only known, I would have done whatever it took to make him happy.

To those of you out there who have dreams and have a list in their head, share them with your parents, don't hide them. Maybe they will become reality, but only if others know. Only if I had known…

The one entry that hurts me inside is Learn to surf. He did tell me about this desire to learn to surf recently and we did act on it. Andrew and I were planning to go to Mexico this past summer to learn surfing, but his broken right hand got in the way and we could not make the trip. Before I left Boulder the last time I saw him, we talked about going to Mexico during his winter break and he was excited and happy to do that. It would have been our time together for a week or so, just Dad and Andrew living on the beach, learning to surf, taking some pictures, and doing what dads and their sons do. I will forever miss that opportunity.

THREE THINGS THAT MADE ANDREW WHO HE WAS
February 20, 2014

PART I

WHEN ANDREW WAS about eleven or twelve and Nicole about nine, Lonya came by the house the week before Purim and gave them each a small basket of Purim treats, a Purim Basket. I had known Lonya for years, from playing hockey, and she had met and talked to my kids several times at the various rinks we played in. The bags contained some hamentashen cookies, candy, and small gifts, part of a Jewish tradition known as mishloach manot. Basically it is a mitzvah, making sure people have enough food for the Jewish holiday of Purim, but also a mitzvah to give charity, especially to children. Although Nicole was eager to accept the gift unconditionally, and loved the cookies and gifts, the gift puzzled Andrew. He had met Lonya only a few times, he was not close friends with her, he did not celebrate Purim other than in Hebrew school, and he had never received a gift before that was not associated with something he related to his birthday, Chanukah, or Christmas. He did, of course, eat everything and play with the toys, but he thought about it a lot.

He stored it in the back of his mind for years. Every once in a while, he would ask me about it and ask how Lonya was doing. Over the years, he bought small items with the intention of donating them to someone who could not afford them. He routinely donated his unused toys and clothes to the needy, even asking Nicole for her unused toys to donate. This became something that he did throughout his life. Even in Boulder, instead of throwing stuff away, he would bring it to a donation site and leave it there in hopes that someone would find it and use it.

I thank Lonya for teaching Andrew this valuable life lesson that changed his way of thinking. You touched and affected my son's life in a very positive manner, and for that I am forever thankful.

PART II

A year or so later (and I am sorry to have to make this into a hockey story), while Andrew was talking to me in the car ride home from a game, he mentioned that one of the players on his team, Robert (not his real name), was tying a pair of hockey socks around his shoulders to give the appearance under his jersey that he was wearing shoulder pads. He didn't know why, neither did I. All I knew was that Robert came from a family that did not have the means to buy a lot of nice things, that he received a scholarship to play hockey with the organization, and that when we traveled he stayed in another player's room to save money. I figured it was for financial reasons that he used the socks —he could not afford a new set of shoulder pads. Thinking about it, Robert also had ratty old gloves, and skates that were too small for him.

In a day or two I talked to my young son again and told him why Robert had the socks, and that he should not mention it in the locker room, so as to not embarrass him—it probably already bothered him that the other players knew, but let's not bring it up. Andrew's immediate response to me was that he could give his pads to Robert and we could go out and buy some new ones. Andrew always loved new equipment. Although a good idea, I told him that his would not fit Robert—Andrew was about 140 pounds, Robert about 180. He didn't let it go and pushed me more. He asked if any of the Manhattanville players that we were friends with had old pads that they didn't want—they get new equipment in college. I wasn't sure, but I would ask. It took a little while, but eventually Andrew's coach, Coach Rich, did get used, and some new, equipment from Manhattanville, and Robert got nice new equipment, including skates, to replace the only equipment he could afford.

Andrew learned a lesson from this, and learned compassion for others through Robert. I also have to thank Coach Rich for stepping in, seeing a need, and using his contacts and friendships to help out tremendously. It might have seemed a small thing back then, but it shaped how Andrew thought from then on.

PART III

Andrew's neurologist, Dr. Roseman, ran a coat drive for disadvantaged youth in and around Westchester for several years. Andrew cleaned out his closet and found a few coats to donate, he felt pretty good about that. But when we were at a rink that weekend and he saw a dozen or so unclaimed coats in the lost and found, he asked me about them. If you have ever been in a rink, there is always a box somewhere called the lost and found, and it is always overflowing with jackets, hats, gloves, skates, etc. Most things in the box are never claimed and eventually thrown away. We talked to the rink manager who showed us the back room where he had about twenty unclaimed kids' coats that were going to be thrown away soon. The smile on Andrew's face when he asked if we could have them to donate and was told yes was priceless. He got a couple of bags to pack them all into and filled the back of my truck. This turned into Andrew's Bar Mitzvah project.

This repeated itself at almost every rink we went to from November through January. All in all, Andrew collected over a hundred and fifty children's coats, bagged them, and stored them in our garage. Finally, in January, we brought them over to Dr. Roseman to give out to the needy. I was happy to have my garage back, and Andrew was so thrilled when he got a hug and a huge thank you from the doctor.

Thank you, Dr. Roseman, for giving Andrew a project that he turned into a mission.

FINALLY

This was Andrew. He was compassionate and constantly thought about others. He did not have a lot of material possession, he did not keep stuff he had no use for, and he did not really collect anything. He used what he needed and gave the rest away (other than computer stuff and gaming systems and games, which he had way too much of).

Last summer he asked me for a computer for a friend of his, I didn't even recognize the name. He said his friend's mother did not have a job and she was going to the library to use their computer to find a job, and that they could not afford a computer. I had a spare unused computer in the house which he asked for. Andrew cleaned out that computer, reformatted it, reinstalled Windows and all the drivers and Microsoft Office, and set up that computer in their house. He also punched a hole through the wall so they could connect it to their neighboring apartment's internet (with their permission of course). He was very happy to help them out, but told only me, never made it public or told his other friends. He never wanted the attention, he just wanted to help out.

I share these stories for a few reasons. One is that it shows a lot about Andrew. What shaped his thinking, and how he reacted to what he heard and saw in life. Second is to thank those who shaped his life in a positive manner, without knowing it or asking for it, though they had a very positive influence on Andrew. And third, so that when we start Andrew's foundation this spring, you will know why we are doing what we are doing in his name, in his memory, and in his honor.

If you experienced Andrew's generosity, his thoughtfulness, his compassion, his charity, everyone would greatly like to hear about it. Please post a comment, even anonymously, but share with others so everyone can see what Andrew was all about.

Thank you.

I STILL HAVE TWO CHILDREN
February 25, 2014

WHAT I HAVE to think about and be grateful for in my life is my daughter, Nicole. She is the love of my life, she is the bright spot in my life, she keeps me going each and every day. And I do say *think about,* because I have to constantly remember that I have another child. One that is still with us, one that I deeply and truly love as much as I have ever loved Andrew, one that I talk to and text as much as I can. I know that sounds hard to understand, but there is a real difference in my love for my children.

I speak to Nicole about once a week, we text each other a couple of times a week, and I get to see her about every other weekend. I think this is pretty normal for a college kid. I have her pictures on my desktop, on the wall next to my desk, and in the living room. I love watching her play hockey, taking rides with her to go shopping, and going out to her favorite restaurants. I look forward to her graduating college, getting married, and having children, my grandchildren. I love to hear about what is going on in her life, she asks me to do her favors or take care of things for her. I look forward every day to growing older and watching my precious daughter grow into a young woman, get a job, maybe coach one day. This is what I live for every single moment. She is nineteen now, she will be twenty-two when she graduates from college, maybe twenty-eight or thirty when she gets married, and thirty or thirty-five when she has a child. There are so many new memories I look forward to making with my daughter. She will also, as she so often reminds me, pick an old age home to put me in one day. She is here, she is physically with us, she is my child who forever will be in my arms.

Andrew is twenty-one. He was twenty-one last August, he was still twenty-one two months after his last birthday in December. Next year he will be twenty-one. When I turn fifty-five and sixty and six-five, he will still be twenty-one. With Andrew, I have to recall the years we had together. The times we went SCUBA diving, the times we worked on his car together. I have to remember our ski trips and how much he loved to snowboard and how we used to make and eat sushi for dinner. All I have for my dear beloved only son

is memories and photographs of him. And I worry, as I get older, will the memories fade? I will never forget his laughter or his love for our Labradors Daisy and Daphne—every morning when he arose (sometimes around noon) he would go and lay down on my bed and hug them and pet them and tell them he loved them—they looked forward to that special time. I remember…him putting this set of fake wax lips in his mouth that Nicole got in a gift to make us all laugh in the car.

I remember how we would be on a boat after SCUBA diving and he would talk about the amazing colors of the fish and the vast openness and textures of the coral. And he loved to eat. I would watch how he would eat this amazing gelato that Nicole brought home from Via Vanti, it was probably his favorite treat in the world and it was like an out-of-body experience to watch him eat it and guess the flavors. He loved The Cheesecake Factory and P.F. Chang's, and asked me to cook items from their menus when he was home—which I was more than glad to do. I remember him being adventurous with his food, as well. When we went out for my birthday a couple of years ago to my favorite Peruvian restaurant, he ordered skewered cow heart with onions and fries. It was amazingly good. I remember him smiling when he came off the ice after each and every ice hockey game he

played in—win or lose. I remember him making his friends and teammates laugh in the locker before and after games—even his coaches laughed. He would sneak into pictures I was taking for my eBay clients--more than once. This is what I have of my son—memories. There are no new memories, there are no new birthdays, there are no new pictures. I still cannot believe he is really gone. He is the child that will forever be in my heart.

I hope that people can understand and somehow accept this. Yes, we do still have two children, and always will.

"One child is forever in my arms, and the other is forever in my heart."

And they were and always will be best friends.

IS MY SON AT PEACE—REALLY?
March 2, 2014

ONE THING I am having a hard time with is the question "Is Andrew at peace?"

I speak to people all the time about Andrew and generally everyone says Andrew is in a better place. They say he is in heaven, and that he is at peace. He is with G-d, he is with my father whom he never met before, and he is with Poppy, whom he loved and cared for dearly. He is with all those who passed before him that he never had the chance to meet, as well as those he did know during the short period of time that was his life. They say that in heaven, you are happy, you are at total peace, everything is peaceful, you have no worries, you are in paradise.

People generally also say that he is with us, all of us—Dorothy, Nicole, me. He is with Grandma, Bubby, Greg and Todd, Wally and Matt, Jovi and Jay. He is here, he is watching over us, he is taking care of us. He gives us signs and protects us, all while being at peace in heaven.

But I have a question. One that has haunted me for months. One that I am just stuck on.

Andrew can see the pain and grief that we are all going through. He can see Dorothy crying herself to sleep, or waking up in the middle of the night crying. He can see me crying in my office every single day, finding it hard to concentrate and focus. He can see how we are struggling to make it through day by day without him. He can feel how his closest friends miss him and pain for him. He sees Grandma crying for him in church every day. He sees all of this pain that his passing has caused on this earth. How can he be happy and at peace with all this pain here on earth, wherever his soul is now?

I know that he did not cause his own passing, he took what he was told to take by his doctors. I know it was a medical issue that no one could have foreseen and no one could have prevented. It was not his fault, it was not the doctors' fault, it was not anyone's fault, he just died. He went to sleep, and very peacefully his life ended. It just ended. I don't blame him for his passing, no one does—I love him too much for that. No one blames anyone, it just happened.

But how can he really be at peace? He must be in pain, crying himself, just to see all of us in so much pain. He is such a sensitive being, such a sensitive soul, how can he just not be affected by the pain here on earth and be at peace as everyone says he is. I love him so much, and I want him to be at peace, I want his time in heaven to be peaceful and I want all those good things I hear about heaven to be so for my son.

How can we do this, how can we make this happen? I don't know. Maybe no one knows. You see movies like Ghost, and realize maybe it is letting him go, to bring him peace. I read poems like the ones below and think about letting go, if I can. Maybe we have to learn from his passing, maybe we have to look at what he had and be thankful. But what is letting go? I can't just let go of my son. I can't let go of his hand, I can't let go of holding on to him in my thoughts. I will never let him go—but do I need to? Do I need to figure out how to let him go and start to live my life again? Would that be disrespectful to his memory? I know he would want me to go on and live my life and still love and respect his memory.

We will never forget him, we can't. We will never stop looking at his pictures or telling stories about him. His face, his voice, the way he smells after a shower, his love will never ever be forgotten. Not by just us, but, as I hope and expect, many will always remember him. But maybe I can learn to let go of his hand. Maybe I can learn to let go of his collar and let him move to a place he needs to be in to be at peace. And maybe that will let me move to a place I can be at peace as well. I just don't know.

I have to think more, open myself up more, and eventually write more about this when I figure it out. This is just the beginning.

These are all poems/images, originally viewed on Facebook, that I have read and make me think.

I'm Free

Don't grieve for me, for now I'm free,
I'm following the path God laid for me.
I took his hand when I heard his call,
I turned my back and left it all.

I could not stay another day,
To laugh, to love, to work, to play.
Tasks left undone must stay that way,
I've found that peace at the close of the day.

If my parting has left a void,
Then fill it with remembered joy.
A friendship shared, a laugh, a kiss,
Ah yes, these things I too will miss.

Be not burdened with times of sorrow,
I wish you the sunshine of tomorrow.
My Life's been full, I savored much,
Good friends, good times, a loved one's touch,

Perhaps my time seemed all too brief,
Don't lengthen it now with undue grief.
Lift up your heart and share with me,
God wanted me now, He set me free.

Author Unknown

I am Still Here

Friend, please don't mourn for me
I'm still here, though you don't see.
I'm right by your side each night and day
and within your heart I long to stay.

My body is gone but I'm always near.
I'm everything you feel, see or hear.
My spirit is free, but I'll never depart
as long as you keep me alive in your heart.

I'll never wander out of your sight—
I'm the brightest star on a summer night.
I'll never be beyond your reach—
I'm the warm moist sand when you're at the beach.

I'm the colorful leaves when fall comes around
and the pure white snow that blankets the ground.
I'm the beautiful flowers of which you're so fond,
The clear cool water in a quiet pond.

I'm the first bright blossom you'll see in the spring,
The first warm raindrop that April will bring.
I'm the first ray of light when the sun starts to shine,
and you'll see that the face in the moon is mine.

When you start thinking there's no one to love you,
you can talk to me through the Lord above you.
I'll whisper my answer through the leaves on the trees,
and you'll feel my presence in the soft summer breeze.

I'm the hot salty tears that flow when you weep
and the beautiful dreams that come while you sleep.
I'm the smile you see on a baby's face.
Just look for me, friend, I'm everyplace.

Author Unknown

Sometimes the most productive thing you can do is rest
and let your angels wrap you in their loving wings.
They've got you covered.

Reprinted with permission: EmilyQuotes.com

THE LAST WORDS
March 8, 2014

THIS IS A little bit different from my normal posts. It is not about Andrew, or our loss of him. It is about the last words, the final words. The other night at our bereavement group, one of the mothers who lost her boy last year was terribly upset. She cried and sobbed over the loss of her son openly. But, really,  what bothered her and gave her grief were the last words they spoke. He apparently did some physically toiling, sweaty work outside and was going out that night with friends without showering. She asked him to shower, she implored him to, but all he said was that he did not care and was late for his friends—he twisted his baseball cap around and headed out the door. As he was running out, she verbally expressed her disappointment with him, quite specifically and expressively, and he was gone. Not just gone from the house that night, but gone from her life forever—he passed without making it home that night.

And all she could think about, and what she has to live with the rest of her life was that last remark, that last sentence, that last voice of frustration. And it burns inside of her and is a constant terrible source of pain and anguish. She could not take the words back, she cannot now or ever explain those words. And she is not alone.

Another family we know had a similar situation. I do not recall the exact situation, nor what led to the friction, nor who said what last, but that there were words said, feelings hurt, and their son left the house, left his home, and they did not talk for weeks afterward—each waiting for the other to break the silence, each waiting for the other to maybe apologize, each waiting for the other to grow up. But that never happened. Their son passes as well—the silence never broken, but now the silence is forever. The frustration over those last words is forever.

We talked about this and two points came up.

One thing you can take from this is that your children are your most precious things in life. How can you fight with them and let it go unresolved? How can you let them leave the house frustrated, upset, mad? You never know if the words will be your last. I have heard many times that one of the secrets to a long-lasting, happy marriage is that you never go to bed upset or mad at your spouse. Then how can you possibly let your child, who is so much more fragile and sensitive than your spouse, leave you when they are upset. How can you let them turn and walk away? How can you not call them or text them or reach out to them and offer a resolution, so that you may both go to sleep happy—never knowing if it is the last time they will go to sleep.

Can you live the rest of your life with what you said to them the last time they left your side?

But—we are also parents. We have to nurture and encourage them. We have to guide them and teach them. We have to set them straight when they drift, we have to discipline them when they break the rules, and we have to treat them like adults when they act like babies. That sometimes includes saying things to them that might hurt, that might offend or bother them, that may include raising our voices to them, it might include walking out of the room and not giving in. That is all about being a parent and raising good, compassionate, trustworthy, righteous children. No parent can raise a child without discipline, without being a parent, without ruffling a few feathers now and again. Without pissing off our dearly loved children once in a while. And then walking away to let our children think about it, and, as we hope, come to the right decision using the tools that we provided them with during their upbringing.

That is the potential quandary that every parent faces. The two parents I mentioned above know that what they did was right. They have come to peace with themselves and what happened between them and their sons. They know that they were being parents— good parents. They know what they did was right for their child. They know that their boys are not resentful or upset where they are now. They know that their boys are at peace with themselves and with their parents. But it still hurts. It hurts like hell knowing that the last conversation was not one of love and happiness but, rather, one of being a parent.

Every time your child walks away from you, every time he or she leaves the house, every time you say goodbye, every time you hang up that phone, think about it. Are you being their friend? Are you being their mother or father? Are you being a disciplinarian? Are they leaving you upset and is there cause for that upset? Or did you just have a bad day at work and take it out on them? And, a minute later, maybe in an hour, maybe in a day, can it be repaired?

Is there an answer? Absolutely not. It is good that almost none of you will pre-decease your children, and that people will pass in the correct order. But as I write this, I come across another thought. What do you want your children's last thoughts of their parents to be? What do you want the last conversation that you have with your children to be about? How do you want it to end? So when you walk away, walk into that bright light, what will they remember?

About remembering— I remember that when I was sixteen my father drove me to school in the dead of winter. We talked about the lawn and about the garden coming back in spring. We smiled and laughed. He pulled up to the school, drove to the last door, I leaned over, kissed him goodbye, and got out of the car. I was happy, but my father never saw the spring. But I was happy. I am at peace.

WHY? WHY MINE?
March 14, 2014

ANDREW WAS A great kid—really. He was fun to be around, he smiled all the time, never talked ill about anyone, always saw the positive side of life. So why did G-d take him from us? Why did G-d decide not to let our son live out his years on earth with us? Tyler, as well—a great high school student who was taken way too early. And Mark and Kaitlyn, Jeffrey and Patrick, and so many more.

This is the ultimate question that every parent asks when they lose a child: "Why did G-d choose to take my child and not the next one? Why did He not let my son live to be a ripe old man, live to let him see his children married, and live to enjoy his grandchildren? We see bad people, thieves, murderers, ungrateful people, users, wife-beaters, and they live their whole lives out, maybe some of it in jail, but they get the opportunity to live. They get to be alive for so many years. Any yet, our children do not. And all we want to know is why."

When they are taken, they leave such a void, they leave such pain and anguish behind. How can G-d watch the funeral of a child and then take another child. How can He see the mother of a twenty-one-year-old throw herself on her only son's casket crying and yet turn a blind eye and take another son from another mother? How can he watch the baby who lives only seven hours, held by his parents the whole time, read to, talked to, and then take that baby and move on. How does He do this time after time?

Was it my fault? Was it something I said or did sometime that caused this? Did I upset Him, or did I not live a good pious life, was I not enough of a mensch, did I not give enough charity? Parents always ask this and dread that it was their fault.

To those parents who ask that, as well as myself, that is a question we can actually answer. No. And it took me, as well as many others, a while to come to that conclusion. You are not being punished, you did not cause your child's death by upsetting the Almighty. No matter what you said, what you thought, what you did or didn't do, you didn't cause it, you had no control over it. Even if I did something wrong, and G-d decided  to punish me—He would have to look around and see the consequences of His action. If He were punishing a single person, then the collateral damage would not be so widespread and devastating. He would have to see Bubby and Grandma, Andrew's grandmothers, crying and grieving so hard every single day. He would have to see the pain that his cousins are in from losing such a happy part of their family. He would have to see his mother unable to sleep at night, and crying whenever she thinks of her dear sweet son she held in her arms not so many years ago. How could G-d punish one person, and cause so much grief to others? Don't blame yourself—as we have learned not to blame ourselves. It is a long, hard road to travel to realize this and to understand it, but it is a road that we all must travel in order to be at peace with the question of Why.

The other answer to this is faith. I know Andrew is in a different place now. I don't know where, I don't know why, I know nothing of it. But I have faith that he is somewhere. He is with his loved ones who passed before him. He is talking to Poppy about the garden. He is talking to Keith about college. He is talking to my father, telling him how his son turned out. I am sure he is arguing with Einstein about something he missed. But I know in my heart he is somewhere. I don't know why I think this, but it is faith. It brings me peace, it brings us all peace.

If there was nothing, just a body that died, and that my son was buried, and we put up a headstone one day and that is it, then it would hurt so much more. If he just died and nothing of his essence, nothing of his soul, nothing of his compassion moved on, then I would be devastated. But I know that this is not the case. I know he moved on, he left his body, he left that dark hole in the ground and moved somewhere else. All that I taught him, all that he knew about helping others and all that was him had to end up somewhere, and he had to take that all with him. All I have is my faith that that has happened. As we all have that faith in anyone who has moved on. They have simply moved to another dimension, another level of consciousness, another place that we cannot understand yet. But they are somewhere, and we can rest easy knowing that. We can live out the rest of our lives knowing that one day we will be with them again and we will hug them and talk to them again. One day we might understand more. And that brings us peace and enables us to let go. It enables us to talk about them, to relish the lives they had, and to know we are okay.

You ask—Why? I answer, Because we have the faith to let them go. We have the faith that they are somewhere and that they are at peace. That is all I can offer.

You ask—Why mine? I can't answer that. But I can tell you it was not your fault. There was nothing you could do to save them. There was nothing you did that caused them to pass. You have the faith and strength to believe that—truly believe that.

If you agree, if you do have the faith, if you are at peace, please leave a comment and let others know—it truly helps so many. If you know someone who blames themselves, please pass this on to them in the hope that it will help them.

I'VE LEARNED TO LISTEN DIFFERENTLY
March 23, 2014

A FEW WEEKS ago I was with a colleague, Sara (not her real name), who lost an employee in a car accident. This employee and Sara had grown pretty close over the few years he worked for her, and she was understandably pretty upset when he passed. We were talking for a few minutes when she said that she knew how I felt losing Andrew, and went on to tell me about the death of her employee, and how it was similar to my losing Andrew. She told me how he called her mom sometimes because she had taken him in and taught him so much. I just smiled, wished her a lovely day and left, as my business was done.

I was pretty freakin' livid. I think you can understand why. She compared her employee of three years, no relationship, not family, nothing, and losing him in a car crash, to the loss of my son, my only son, of twenty-one years. Was she that disingenuous that much removed, so lacking in understanding as to make this comparison? I went across the street to another client, who happens to be a very close friend and told him what had happened. He was as upset as I was, he stood in the same corner as I in thinking, How could she possibly be so removed from reality as to make this comparison? It took a few weeks to get this out of the front of my mind, but I eventually moved on, until I told the story to Rich, a coach with whom I have been friends and a teammate for many years.

He heard a different conversation with Sara than I had heard. And he expressed it to me and told me what he thought of what she said. He actually made me think about not what she said but why she said it. Not about the content, but the cause. And it hit me, maybe I was just not listening the right way.

Sara was reaching out to me in any way she could. She had not experienced the loss of her own child, thankfully. But she wanted to say something and connect to me in some way, and this was her attempt to do so. She meant no harm by it, didn't mean to hurt me or to compare herself to me, and, more importantly, didn't mean to minimize my loss. It was just a way of her reaching out to me in my grief and connecting to me in some way.

I look at that conversation very differently now. Although it still hurts when people compare their loss of a cousin, or their parent, or a young friend, to the loss of my son, I now realize that it is done innocently and they are attempting to help me. Thank you.

In the same vein as this, there are also the times I have to hear people say that we are strong, that we are strong to survive this tragedy. And the same lesson I have learned above helps us get through that comment. If you have made that comment to us, please do not be offended, we so much appreciate hearing that, and we really appreciate that you are reaching out to us.

But—we are not that strong. We cry every day. We find it hard to eat a meal and enjoy it because we feel guilty. We don't ever feel like going out, we just want to stay home and be with each other and Nicole. Some of our friends are taking us out for lunch or dinner, and that is really good for us and we so much enjoy going out with them. We get to talk to them about life and have a nice meal with them. Not because we are strong, but because we need to. Not because we are strong, but because we need to live and to talk about Andrew, and remember him with others. Not because we are strong, but because we have no choice.

We are still here. Nicole is still here. Our mothers and nephews and niece are still here. We need to work and eat and live some sort of life. Yes, it takes strength to get out of bed every morning, and some days we just can't. Some days after work we go to bed after dinner, turn off the phones, shut down e-mail, and leave everyone alone because we just don't have the strength to do anything or talk to anyone. But we know there is tomorrow, and we have to get up, go to work, talk to people and, much as I hate to say it, be strong.

Are we strong? Is everyone who has lost a child and is still functioning, strong? Or are we just surviving, and the strength that we get from our lost children to continue living our lives makes us appear to be strong?

I know I find strength to keep going from Andrew and Nicole and Dorothy. I know my son wants me to live my life and to enjoy life, and do the things he and I never got to do together, even as he has left me. I know that Nicole brings me strength and love every single day by being there for me, by telling me how much she enjoys life and college, and how much she is looking forward to things in the future. Events that I want to and need to be here for. And I find strength from Dorothy seeing how she is handling this day by day, how she still manages to go to work every day and function, and how she still cares for her mom all the time. I also find strength in writing my journal, which I hope is helping people, not just those of us who have suffered the worst loss imaginable but, as well, those of you who try to relate to us, try to reach out to us and be

Andrew playing with Peanut at CU Boulder

our friends—I hope my journal opens your eyes to what we are going through and how much you are helping us. That is where my strength comes from.

He actually let me take these pictures while he was relaxing and chasing Peanut

He found great joy in animals, and loved the unconditional love Peanut provided

DOES SHE REMEMBER?
March 27, 2014

I LOOK AT her in her eyes and ask her if she misses Andrew.

She looks back at me emotionless with her brown eyes.

I ask her if she remembers playing with him every single morning.

I ask her if she remembers all the joy that he brought her and that she brought him.

She stares back at me, maybe tilting her head.

I ask her if she cries over Andrew like I do every single day.

I ask her if she is sad at all for not having Andrew around anymore.

She stares back at me and wags her tail.

That is all she knows.

Sometimes I am jealous of Daphne in that respect. She feels no sadness, no remorse, no pain. Her memory is but a brief time  period. Does she remember the times she ran and played with Andrew out in the snow? Does she remember swimming with him in the lake, or pulling the paddle boat while we all laughed and cheered her on?

Does she remember how much he loved her and Daisy. That he cried all night when Daisy passed, just a few brief weeks before Andrew passed. We were all so devastated. Whenever Andrew called home, he always asked how the dogs were—then he would ask us everything else. The first thing he did when he got home was to sit and play with them for such a long time—then out with his friends, and they would wait for him by the window at night. They would often sleep

with him that first night, even on the floor, they were so happy their friend had come home. They sat outside his door and waited for his leftovers when he ate dinner at two in the morning. We would often find plates in the hallway—perfectly clean.

When we traveled, Andrew and Nicole always brought them food from breakfast—way too much, but they loved it and ate

every morsel. From French toast to eggs to crumb cake to donuts—nothing was off limits for their special travel breakfasts. We never had to ask twice for someone to take them out, both kids where eager to walk them and run with them. Andrew had pictures of them on his desk, and on his phone and on his computer background. They were such a part of his life. I have so many pictures of Andrew and Nicole with the dogs and cats, we can never forget them. Daisy was also my best friend and companion.

When we did our last family holiday card, the last one when we were a full family, Daisy and Daphne got included, instead of

Mom and Dad, but we were happy—everyone in the picture was so happy. You can see the love in all of their eyes.

We don't have Daisy any-more. As some of you know, she is with Andrew now, buried in his arms, next to his heart. I am sure they are playing and running and sleeping together wherever they are. Maybe wait-ing for Daphne to join them again someday.

But does she know? I don't think so. She is blessed with a short memory, she does not cry over him, she does not miss him. Sometimes she goes into his room and sniffs around, jumps on his bed, smells his clothes, but then wags her tail and carries on. Life is so simple and happy for her. Feed her, walk her, play with her, love her—that is all she needs—and that is what the kids gave her—unconditional love.

Sometimes I am jealous of Daphne, she has no sorrow, she has no pain.

But I also feel sorry for her, I sometimes pity her. She does not remember the love and the compassion and the friendship that Andrew gave her and that she gave him. She does not have those amazing memories of them playing in the snow or in the lake. She does not remember my son. I don't think I would be able to go on if I did not have so many memories that keep my son alive.

I sit here and cry and look at her—and she just wags her tail and tells me she loves me.

I USED TO ...
April 4, 2014

I USED TO worry about him, where he was, what he was doing, who he was with. Is he okay?

Now I cry over him. I don't see him anymore, I can't call him, I can't hug him. I don't know where he is.

I used to wonder what he would be when he grew up, what would he do for a living. Would he be successful, would he enjoy his career, would he take over my business—eventually. Like every other parent I was concerned with where was he going to end up in life.

Now I only think about what he was like when he was a little boy. I think about his birthday parties and his hockey. I think about what he used to enjoy, the toys that he used to play with, and I hold some of his things that he left behind in my hands, and cry.

I used to call him Thor mostly, sometimes Booboo, and sometimes Andrew. He was my son, my one and only son. I would tell him he was my son, and that I was very proud of everything he did and everything he accomplished, as my father was of me.

I find it hard to even say his name now without crying.

I used to think about what he loved and enjoyed doing and his passions. Where he wanted to travel to—Italy, Israel, Amsterdam. Where he would go snowboarding in the future, where his kids would learn to ski, where he would settle down and call home. I think about next summer, when we planned to go to Mexico to learn to surf together.

Now all I can think about is what he will be missing, and what he will never get to do, because his life was cut so short. The things that my son will never experience.

I used to have stuff in my office that had to be sent to him, a pair of sunglasses, a computer cable, headphones, and clothes. He always

Andrew's colorful collection

liked receiving packages. Whatever I sent him made him happy.

Now I keep his most treasured personal stuff on my desk—the headphones he always used, a set of rocks and gems he was collect-

ing in Boulder for me because he knew I loved them, his colorful gauges (sort of earrings) that he changed every day, his huge assortment of tongue barbells and balls he loved to show off in pictures, and his wallet.

I keep his glasses nearby because that is what he looked through to

see the world, he saw the world in his own unique way--we all remember him in his Ray-Bans. These were the things that made Andrew, Andrew. I look at them every day and they make me smile and remind me

of him. They remind me he had a full, happy, colorful life.

I should be shopping for a suit to wear to his graduation next month, talking to him about a school ring, and framing his diploma. Hugging him as he moves on to the next phase of his life with the whole world ahead of him.

Instead, I am writing down his Hebrew name and shopping for his headstone, something a father should never have to do. Hoping what we pick out he would have liked.

I just miss my Booboo so much, he touched so many lives in positive ways and he will be so missed by so many people.

But, as with all of my fellow grieving parents, as we say so often, I choose to continue. I choose to get up every day, get out of bed, and continue on with my life. I choose to live on despite the overwhelming grief. I choose to spend great quality time with Nicole. I can even choose once in a while to laugh, to have a good time, to enjoy a nice glass of wine, or enjoy a nice dinner with friends. Nicole chooses to carry on and play hockey and wear his jersey number. We choose to live on in Andrew's honor, in his memory. I carry him with me everywhere I go, in everything I do, and every word I speak, He is always with me and on my mind, but I do choose to carry on knowing that that is what he would want me and Dorothy and Nicole to do.

He didn't have a choice, he was taken without warning or say. But those of us left behind do have a choice, and Andrew, as well as all of our lost children, would want us to live on and enjoy our lives—despite the grief. We will never forget them, ever. The hole in our hearts never ever mends. But we choose to live on in their honor and in their memory—that is the best we can do for them now.

I love you, Andrew.

I love you, Nicole.

Daddy

THERE ARE NO NEW MEMORIES—STORIES OF ANDREW

April 11, 2014

WE OFTEN TELL stories of Andrew—not in the past, but in the present. We often say, "If Andrew were here …" or "You know Andrew would do this or that if he were here." It is our way of holding on to the memories of him as well as keeping him in the forefront of our minds, as he always is.

Just last week, Dorothy and I went to Smashburger in White Plains for the first time. Yeah, we had a moment of weakness and desired a good juicy burger. It brought back the memory that one of the last lunches I had with Andrew and Jovi was at the Five Guys in Boulder, it was the first time any of us had been to a Five Guys, although we passed  it hundreds of times. We were amazed at the size of the burgers and took pictures of them, and of ourselves, and sent them to Dorothy. We had a good time that meal, talked about Boulder and what a good time we had had for the past week or so together.

Back at Smashburger, they gave us our food and the receipt, and on the bottom of the receipt the cashier pointed out that if we went on-line with our smartphone and filled out a short survey, we could get a free side. So we casually ate, talked about Nicole and Andrew, and filled out the survey and got the code, and I went up for our free side. To my surprise, I got the receipt for the side, amount due was $0, but on the bottom of the new receipt was a chance to fill out another survey and get another free side!

OK, now for those of you who knew Andrew, tell me that this would not start a long hilarious challenge for him to accumulate an entire large bag full of free sides? Can't you just see him saying, This is so stupid—as he fills out another survey and gets another free side order and another receipt with the survey on it? I could picture Matt or Wally or Todd sitting at the table as Andrew piled up the free sides. Dorothy and I sat there, smiled and laughed as we thought about what our dear little boy would do.

I hope this brings a smile to someone's face just picturing him going back to get his numerous free sides, as he laughs and shakes his hands in disbelief. It brought one to our faces for a time. That was Andrew.

I got this message from Andrew back in August, 2011—it shows his compassion and how he really loved animals:

"Dad—hi can you do me a favor, well it's for my friend's

dog June who is 1 and a half and has a birth defect and needs another surgery that his family doesn't think they can afford its real expensive, http://www.giveforward.com/savejune-bug, that's the site for his dog, a lot of our friends are donating a little to him and I wanted to give him something for her, I really like her and it's the right thing to do. he's also giving me a set of trucks for free for the other long board that I have so I can use it when I'm home, he didn't want any money for them just for me to donate to June. http://www.facebook.com/pages/Save-June-Bug/137368123019122 that's the page on Facebook that you should like and if you can post something on Facebook with or about it so people see, you have friends that would care about it, or possibly donate, there were a lot of anonymous donations on that site.

Thanks
Love you"

We of course donated to help June. Unfortunately, on August 27, 2011, Junebug passed away. Andrew called me from school and told me—he was very upset and I could hear it in his voice. We talked awhile about our pets and although he was happy to know they were well, the loss of a friend's pet really affected him. He loved Junebug and was upset any time an animal died. This is why one of the charities we chose for him was one to save and protect animals.

He was a funny kid as well. When I posted a picture of me on a motorcycle on Facebook, and said I wasn't really going to buy one, he sent me this text: "oh I know, not only is it about 25k but I know mommy would kill you before the bike does—lol, but its really nice"

We went to see Nicole this weekend and she told us, in a very happy and laughing manner, about her last shopping expedition with Andrew. They went to buy sneakers together, not necessarily the same ones, but they both needed new sneakers. For years, Andrew had worn white sneakers, just white, several different brands, but white. Recently he had changed that to include some colorful ones, for skateboarding, and because he lived in Boulder, where everyone has some color of some sort.

After one or two stores, and looking at dozens and dozens of pairs, none of them fit what he was looking for. They ended up in Vans. Nicole described the wall of sneaker choices as massive, the length of the store. Andrew walked up and down the wall and looked and looked, picked up a few pairs, inspected them, and returned them to the shelf—Nicole all this time losing patience. He would pick up a pair, look at it from every angle and imagine how he would look in them—just like he did with flannel shirts and blue jeans. This went on for some time, it seems like hours the way Nicole describes it.

He finally picked out a pair—and with all the choices, all the colors, patterns, laces, he picks out a solid gray pair of sneakers. He tries them on and looks at himself from every angle in the mirror to make sure they make the right statement about him. We are never sure what that statement is, but I guess they made it because he bought that gray pair. And to our surprise, Nicole purchased the same pair.

I am not sure if it came with sneakers or not, but they also got matching Vans T-shirts. So the sneakers and T-shirts matched—which, I think, was the very first time that they actually bought something that matched. But I guess something caught Andrew's eye, and, never one to pass up the opportunity to buy something computer-related, he also bought these cool 4″ square cardboard box PC speakers—I have been using them now for a few months.

I am happy that they had the experience together, and Nicole shared it with us while we all laughed and imagined Andrew walking up and down a row of hundreds of sneakers until he found the pair that he identified with. Solid gray, simple sneakers.

These are just a few memories of Andrew. And unfortunately, there are no new memories of him. What we have in our minds now, what we have pictures of, what we have thought about, that's it. There is nothing new, there will never be any new memories that we experienced with him, the number is set in stone and will forever be.

What we do ask, and we have really never asked his friends for much, is this. If you have a memory or a story or an anecdote or anything about Andrew, can you please post it in the comments below? We would love to add to our memories of him, and to be able to share stories about Andrew that we do not know yet. I know it might be hard, for I am sure it will be hard for us to read, but this will serve as a tribute to him for others to read and share. If it is personal, you can email it to me, or post it anonymously, but please do write something.

Thank you. Dorothy, Nicole, and I really appreciate it.

I don't know how to end this entry of memories.

I just miss my Booboo so much, he touched so many lives in positive ways and he will be so missed by so many people.

I love you, Andrew.
Daddy

THE PATH—AND THE WALL
April 19, 2014

EVERYONE IS ON a path in life, and all of the decisions we make in life change that path, or we can say that the path is created by our decisions. I tend to believe that most people start out on a nice peaceful path, leading to a happy, healthy life. But then reality settles in.

We are a smart species, so we make decisions looking at the long term—we decide to go to the doctor to stay healthy, we decide to go to school or college, get educated, and hope that adds wealth and security somewhere along our path. We hope for love and happiness in the pursuit of marriage and eventually children. But we all make decisions about where we are on the path and where we want our separate paths to lead in life.

And every day, every hour, we walk that path. We put one foot in front of the other and we walk our path, hoping for the best.

This is the bad part. The unexpected part. The unfortunate part. We get ill. Our company goes bankrupt. We get into a serious accident. Our child falls gravely ill. There is a fire. There is a flood.

There is a murderer. And this all affects our perfectly planned-out path. They put road blocks up, diversions, cones, and yield signs on our paths. But we still, day after day, follow that path, hoping for the best, in hope that happiness and joyfulness will be around the next curve in the path. And for most of us, there is.

Then there are those whose feet have stopped. Those who no longer can see the path. The grieving parents of lost children. Our children's paths were much too short, just a few hours long. Some paths, like Derek's, lasted only seven hours. But he was loved and held and read to for his entire life. The mark he left on this world in his short time will never leave or be forgotten. Or Matthew's path, which ended tragically at twenty-one while he was teaching and helping others enjoy the outdoors, which he loved so much. Or Jeff's path, that of an accomplished, gifted, and successful glass blower, which ended on Storrow Drive in a tragic motorcycle accident. Or Andrew's path, my Andrew, whose path ended while he was quietly asleep in his bed. And the list goes on and on, unfortunately. These are the parents whose feet have stopped moving forward. These are the people who have come to a pause in their lives, and on their paths. The pain of knowing that their children's paths have ended is so overwhelming that we—yes, I put myself in that category, we--cannot take another step.

Someone has put a wall in front of us. This is a common story told among grieving parents to those who recently lost a child. There is a wall. A wall of pain, a wall of suffering. A wall so large and onerous that you cannot simply go around it—it is too wide. You cannot go over it—it is too tall. It cannot be dug under or avoided. You must go through it. You might put it off with anger, or depression. But the wall will be waiting for you and you must go through it. For some the wall is narrow, and they can go on and live and love and learn to enjoy life once again. For others the wall never seems to end, and although they are living, they are not really living life. For most of us, we do get through the wall, somehow, but it takes years. But we do learn to live again, love again, and enjoy our lives and embrace what we had on our path before the wall. But it is a lifelong journey along our new path.

But—our feet won't move us sometimes. We can't take the steps to or through the wall. But we all seem to get to the wall, and work our way through it. And it takes years and years to get through the wall and see that there is a glimmer of light on the other side. How do we do this?

As Pam and Georgine put it, there is something, or someone, gently pulling us, gently guiding us along the new path we are on now. Yes, we are moving along the path again, but in a different manner now. Our paths have changed so much, we are such different people now that our feet do not know where to step. We know the path is there, but we can't see it through our tears. So we are pulled delicately down the path by this force. And we willingly let it pull us. We know we must go on, we know we still have a path in life that we must follow, so we let this unknown, caring, loving force gently tug us and pull us along the path.

We rely on this gentle tugging to get us through the day. It is a warming, soothing feeling that we are being helped along. Sometimes our friends hold our hands and help us along the path with their love and friendship. Sometimes our children help us because we know they need us to move. We just follow along the path, day by day, with the smallest of baby steps. The smallest movement forward. Every step is a milestone, every movement is hard, but we keep going.

We know one day our paths will end as well. But on the cusp at the end of our paths, when we look back over our shoulders do we see black clouds, empty frames, and broken cobblestones? Or do we see the other side of the wall that we have gotten through, do we see our friends and family smiling, do we know that we made a difference and that we honored our children's memories and lived out our days the way they would want us to live our lives.

LIFE, LIBERTY, AND ...
April 28, 2014

I WAS IN a different temple last night to say Kaddish for Andrew, and the Rabbi there during the course of his speech talked about what we do in life, and that our life has to have meaning. He said that Life, Liberty, and the Pursuit of Happiness is a great idea, and a great basis for the Declaration of Independence. But then he went on to say that although we all want Life, Liberty, and Happiness,  wouldn't it be better if we had Life, Liberty, and Meaning? He didn't go into that much, he only touched on it and then went on to other subjects, but that thought stuck in my head all night.

Life and Liberty—we all pretty much get what that refers to, and although our thoughts on liberty might all be different, we know what liberty generally means. Whether you are a conservative, liberal, right, left, whatever, we all know what we want in life and we have our definition of liberty. I don't want this to be a political platform, however, so enough said about that.

But meaning. That word hit me and I thought not only about how it related to Andrew but how it related to all of us. How can someone who was taken from us so young, after only twenty-one years, have meaning in their life? How can someone who only lasted on this earth a few years, or a few days have meaning in their life. What is meaning? Is it what Andrew found in his life that affected him and made him who he was? Was it that he became enlightened to some meaning and had some course in his life that was going to have meaning to himself? I don't think so.

For anyone, even someone who makes it to seventy, eighty, or ninety years of age, to have a meaningful life means that they had to affect someone else's life, or many people's lives. They had to give meaning to someone else, or something else, they had to give meaning—not receive meaning.

The Rabbi at my sister's temple, the priest at your church, the kindergarten teacher who taught our children, even Andrew's hockey coach who taught them that the team is a family and will be forever—these are all people who had a meaningful life, they gave some meaning to the people they touched in their lives, they had some positive influence over the people they touched. The volunteer at the animal shelter, the fireman who protects our lives, the people at the food pantry—these people all give of themselves—and in turn they all have meaning in their lives.

But do we all have this meaning? Do some of us just go through life making it from one decade to the next? Do we make money and donate a portion of it and count that as our meaning in life? When someone donates millions of dollars to build a hospital wing—yeah, their  life had meaning. If someone donates $180 to build a well for water in Cambodia (https://www.facebook.com/10Wells), they have meaning in their lives because they did something good that will last for years to come.

How about the couple that has a child and gives that child up to a family that cannot bear children? I think that is one of the best meanings in life that someone could have. Bringing joy to a family by means of a young baby is one of the greatest gifts of all.

Did Andrew have a meaning in life? I think he had so much meaning that one essay can't capture it all. You'll see in my next journal …

He brought joy and happiness to our family. He made others smile and enriched the lives of so many other people. His friends tell us how Andrew would sit and listen to them for hours talk about their lives and their problems, and then when they were done he would respond back to them and make them feel so much better. I am not sure what he said, or how he processed what his friends told him, but he seemed to have a gift of giving some meaningful feedback that made others realize their problems were not so big. This is what he wanted to do in life. This was probably his calling, and definitely his meaning in life.

He also brought love and peace to some people. He rescued some from what would have been not such a nice life. He showed some people that a caring therapist could really help people, and those people are now pursuing a degree in psychology or psychotherapy so that they have meaning in their lives.

G-d puts us all here for a purpose. We have to have some meaning in our lives. There are plenty of people's lives that do not have meaning, or they choose not to have a meaningful life. But most of us do. And we need to have meaning in our lives, it fulfills us. It makes us whole, it gives us satisfaction. We volunteer, we teach, we coach, we donate, we guide, we mentor. We touch other lives. This is meaning.

When we pass, and others look back at the path we chose to take, will they look at that path and say this person was a good person, he was a mensch—he had a meaningful life. When I look at my son's path, I am happy. It was much too short, but it was a meaningful path.

I don't know who said this, I heard it in a video:

"If you're not making someone else's life better, then you're wasting your time."

What will they say when they look at your path? Or mine? More about the meaning of Andrew's life in the next entry…

MY LIFE IS ON TV
May 4, 2014

PAM WAS RECENTLY talking about her life, and how it seems she is watching her life on TV—I can relate to this feeling so deeply. I think we all do to some degree, but with grieving parents it is somewhat different.

We sit here watching TV, we watch our lives, we see ourselves working, cooking, maybe playing golf or hockey. We look at the screen and see what's going on. If we don't like what we are doing, we change the channel, move on, take a nap. We watch how we interact with others, and how we grow and how our families change and evolve. As Pam says, her life is the main story on her own TV right now, as it is for all of us.

But then something happens. Something bad. The red crawl opens up—some emergency-sounding tune plays. We get that red scroll along the bottom of the screen we are watching. An accident, tragedy at sea, an earthquake, hundreds dead, maybe thousands. And it catches our eye and we focus on it. We read the scroll, we concentrate on it and hope it would go faster so we can see more. We change channels in hopes of finding out more information, our focus has gone from TV to the emergency, from our lives on TV to the lives of others on the scroll. We are immersed with the news, it is our only focus. And in an hour or two, or a day or two, the scroll is gone. The news is over, we return to the main screen above, we return to our lives on TV.

And we wait for another scroll, we wait for something else to happen, we live our lives between the red scrolls, but knowing one is never too far away—unfortunately.

But then there are those of us whose red scroll never goes away. The scroll of our children's lives, the scroll of our tears and sorrow. The red scroll that reminds us that our children are gone. That scroll never ever goes away. Doug's scroll is five years long—and has not gone away—it is immensely long and Pam never stops thinking about him. Andrew's scroll is a mere eight months long, but always there.

Whenever we watch the TV of our lives, the red scroll is there. Sometimes it is where it should be, just a small portion of the TV screen. We are able to still have our lives above, and function and go out and enjoy our lives. We can manage when the scroll is where it belongs, we never forget, but we can live. Other times the scroll takes over the screen. It becomes the main story, it becomes CNN or MSNBC or FOX—it is all-consuming, it is the entire TV. Anything and everything else in our lives is minimized while the red scroll becomes and encompasses the entire screen, while the memories of our children so overwhelm us that we have to deal with it over everything else. We cry, we mourn, we even visit their resting places, but we recover. Each and every time we do recover. It does eventually return to the small red scroll at the bottom, but it never--no, it never--disappears. It is there for us to see and for us to remember what we have lost for our entire lives. Sometimes the scroll lets us remember the good times, sometimes it tells us our children are okay now, that their pain is no longer. Sometimes it reminds us of family vacations, the good our children did in their lives, or lets us watch them play sports again. And to tell you the truth, I don't want it to disappear. I never want to be without that scroll, without the constant memory of Andrew, and I am sure Pam is happy the scroll is there as well.

When we awake in the morning, the scroll is there. When we retire for the night—we turn off the TV, we turn out the lights, we

close our eyes—the last thing we see before we sleep is the scroll of
our children's lives.

I never stop thinking about him.
It is like the news crawl that runs at the bottom of the screen.
While my life, the main story,
Plays on the TV above it.

—Pam.

FOR THOSE WHOM I JUST MET (a)

May 16, 2014

FOR THOSE WHOM I have just met …

Although it has been a while, I am meeting new people now. I am seeing friends again, and meeting their friends. I am meeting new clients and vendors, and seeing new faces at the workplaces of the clients I have had for years. I am seeing new people for the first time since my life changed.

It is sometimes hard to meet new people. They want to get to know you. What do you do? Where do you live? Is that your wife? And, inevitably, no matter how much I try to avoid it, no matter how much I pray that it does not come up … Do you have children? The one question that, just by thinking about it, makes me tear. The one question the answer to which is sure not only to ruin my day but also that of those who ask it. You ask it innocently enough, you have the best of intentions of learning more about me, but you have no idea. The can of feelings, the jar of emotions, the Pandora's Box of hurt that you just opened. Opened so innocently.

But it is okay. I need to deal with it, and I need to meet new people and function. Please ask about my daughter, and my son. Please ask about Nicole, as well as Andrew. I may tear up, I may cry, I might even make you feel uncomfortable. But this is who I am now. I want you to be a part of my life, I want you to be a colleague, I want you to be a friend. And if I cry it is not because you said something, or asked me something—it is because I miss my son so much. Don't be afraid to talk to me and mention him for fear that you will remind me of my loss and that will upset me. You can never "remind" me of something that is constantly and continuously on my mind. I also cry when I talk about my daughter, for I love her so much, she means so much to me; and I am so proud of her that I tear up over her as well. That is who I am now.

Please, be my friend. Yes, I am a grieving parent, and at times I show it. Most times I am able to control my emotions and function well. It has been only a short time, and as time goes on I am learning to interact with others better, and to meet new people and talk without long breaks to compose myself. If I walk out of the room, it is not you, it is just that I need to get a breath of fresh air, I need to look up at the sky, I need to be alone with Andrew for a moment. When I return and you feel like hugging and reassuring me, that is fine. It happened to me just this morning, and it felt truly fulfilling and genuine.

It will probably be one of the harder things you can do in your life, but it will also be one of the most rewarding.

FOR THOSE WE JUST MET (b)

FOR THOSE WHOM we, the grieving parents, have just met ….

Although it has been a while, we are meeting new people now. We are seeing our friends again, and meeting their friends. We are meeting new clients, customers, patients, vendors, suppliers, and seeing new faces at their offices, and meeting new people at ours. We are seeing new people for the first time since our lives have changed.

It is sometimes hard for us to meet new people. They want to get to know us. What do you do? Where do you live? Is that your husband or wife? And inevitably, no matter how much we try to avoid it, no matter how much we pray it does not come up … "Do you have children?" The one question that, just by thinking about it, makes us tear. The one question the answer to which is sure not only to ruin my day but also that of those who ask it. You ask it innocently enough, you have the best of intentions of learning more about us, but you have no idea. The can of feelings, the jar of emotions, the Pandora's Box of hurt that you just opened. Opened so innocently.

But it is okay. We need to deal with it, and we need to meet new people and function. Please ask about our children, the ones who are still with us, as well as the ones we have lost. Please ask about them, we love to, and need to, talk about them. We may tear up, we may cry, we might even make you feel uncomfortable. But this is who we are now. We want you to be a part of our lives, we want you to be a colleague, we want you to be a friend. And if we cry it is not because you said something, or asked us something—it is because we miss our lost children so much. Don't be afraid to talk to us and mention our sons and daughters for fear that you will remind us of our loss and that it will upset us. You can never remind us of something that is constantly and continuously on our minds. We cry not only for our lost children but, also, when we talk about the children who are still in our arms, for we love them so much, they mean so much to us; and we are so proud of them, that we tear up over them as well. That is who we are now.

Please, be our friend. Yes, we are grieving parents, and at times we show it. Most times we are able to control our emotions and function well. It has been only a short time for some of us, and others have had years to grieve, and as time goes on, we are learning to interact with others better, and to meet new people and talk without taking long breaks to get our composure back. If we walk out of the room, it is not you but that we need to get a breath of fresh air, we need to look up at the sky, we need to be alone with our children for a moment. When we return and you feel like hugging and reassuring us, that is fine, and it is really appreciated. It happens to us all the time, and it feels truly fulfilling and genuine.

It will probably be one of the harder things you can do in your life, but it will also be one of the most rewarding.

PLANTING FOR SPRING
May 25, 2014

What a temporary beautiful life they lead.

WHILE DOROTHY AND I planted our spring flowers, we were talking about how short-lived the beauty they give us is. We knew that the dozens of plants we planted over the weekend would take root, blossom, grow, spread out a little, give off their beauty for people to enjoy, enhance the beauty and enjoyment of our home, and then wither and die in

late fall—all in a matter of months. But the beauty they provided during the time they are alive is well worth the effort of planting them, weeding, watering, and pruning. All the time knowing that they are doomed during the cold weather, and the cycle of planting and withering is to be repeated next year, and the year after that and so on. But this is what you expect.

This year, however, was different. Usually Dorothy plants with the kids and her mom. I generally like to watch from the deck, iced tea in hand. And it is hard work. There is no one to refill my iced tea so I have to keep getting up from my lounge chair and going inside to refill it myself while my family relaxes and enjoys bonding with each other and bonding with mother earth. But this year we did it alone—Dorothy and I. It was very nice, we talked about what flowers Andrew liked, what flowers Nicole enjoys; and how this summer will be different—so different than any other summer before.

It is just the three of us now. Andrew should have come home a couple of weeks ago. He should have graduated with all of his friends. We should have been proud parents watching him walking down the aisle with that amazing smile that he had on when he graduated from high school. Pictures, dinners, handshakes, and happiness. He should be going to parties and headed off for some well-earned vacation with his friends. But none of that is happening. He should have called Dorothy for Mother's Day, we should have been happily packing him up to come home to start the next chapter of his life.

But our plant is gone. The plant that we nourished, cared for, loved, and encouraged has been ripped from our hearts and our lives. When we plant annuals, we know they will die, we know they have a short life span—that is what we sign up for when we get them. But when we plant our perennials, we expect them to live, and to blossom and grow year after year—just like our children. And when that does not happen it is devastating.

Last summer, Andrew and I purchased a fire pit and set it up on the deck. As I mentioned in earlier posts Andrew and I had many fires there over this past summer. We talked for hours at night about school, about life, about hockey, about almost everything. It was the most amazing summer I had with my son in a long time. College really turned him into a mensch, and a person whom I could talk with more easily. He knew our time together was limited and he would soon be going back to Boulder, so he opened up much more this past summer. He told me about his school teachers in the Psych department that he respected so much, how they were published and how he read their articles and stories and learned from them— and most of all admired them. He found a goal and purpose in life and he was beaming with excitement to be able to graduate and become a therapist and help other people who had anxiety issues. He was such a different person from the boy who left our home three years ago and went off to college.

The fire pit is still there and will always be there. It is known as Andrew's fire pit. The two chairs Andrew and I sat on last summer are still there, facing each other, almost always empty. I bought several planters and planted different colored marigolds next to the pit, it is Andrew's garden. The marigolds were Andrew's favorite flower. I never planted flowers before, but I needed to this year, and probably for many years to come. I needed to do something for my son.

I sit there now, alone, looking at the flowers and the empty chair, recalling what we talked about. It brings a smile to my face knowing how happy he was, and a tear to my eye knowing none of those dreams will ever be fulfilled. How he found his place in life finally, and how he was excited to have such a strong direction in life. I sit and look at the flowers, and I know they will all be dead in a few months. No matter how much I nourish them, no matter how much I care for them and no matter what I do, they will be gone in a few months. It is such a vicious, heart-wrenching cycle.

FAITH
June 1, 2014

WE WENT TO church at Nicole's school a few weeks ago around Easter and while it was very enjoyable and moving, what the priest talked about struck me. He talked about Easter and the resurrection, and focused on death and dying and grieving. The priest began his sermon by saying to a young man in the first row (who did not actually lose a family member), "Congratulations on your mother's death." He said it in almost a happy jovial manner. It really struck us all. He elaborated on it and said that "she is in a better place," she is with the Holy One, she is sitting next to Jesus, in a very peaceful and heavenly place.

What was he thinking about?

"You should be happy where she is." He went on to give a very nice sermon about faith in the afterlife, about the meaning of Easter and the resurrection, and about grieving. What he said was very interesting and we all listened attentively.

I watched the others who were in church with us that day. They nodded their heads in agreement. They smiled and listened attentively. They really were engaged. I could tell from the looks on their faces, the gleam in their eyes, the nodding of their heads, that they found peace in what was being said, and they truly believed.

Now, the fact is that I am Jewish, I did not understand some of what he said, and some of it was out-side of my faith and my belief system. But nevertheless, I found comfort in it. Not so much in the exact words he was saying, but in the belief and faith from the others in the church. I know I wrote about this before, and what he said really hit home. He talked about faith and belief and what keeps us spiritually on the right track.

I go to temple every Friday night to say Kaddish for Andrew. Not because I have to, but because I need to. I really need to. I need to be in a religious place, I need to be around other believers, I need to look at the stained glass, look at the arc containing the Torahs, read out of the prayer book, and hear what the Rabbi has to talk about. I need to listen to others daven and be engulfed in their belief. And I know Andrew is there, along with my father. Not because I see them, or hear them, but because I believe they are there with me when I pray. And I need to feel that to be at peace.

The alter at Andrew's Mass

When people talk to me about Andrew and they tell me he is with Jesus, or the Heavenly Father, or with someone specific in Heaven, I smile. I might not agree with them on a religious basis, but when someone believes what they say, and they say it with true feeling and with honorable intent, then what they say is genu-ine and good; regardless of what the religion is that the words come from.

And that brings me peace and happiness.

You have to have faith in something. You have to believe in something. Hey, we may all be wrong. There might be a fat guy up there named Chuck who is running the show and laughing his ass off right now at how wrong we all are. But that does not matter. When we are here, we have faith that there is something there on the other side, and it is that faith that gets us through trying times, hard times, and motivates us through our lives. It is this faith that we fall back on when we need it, it is this faith that makes us take the next step when our feet just won't move. And it is this faith that we embrace when we celebrate something.

Do you believe in heaven? Do you believe in something on the other side? Is there actually something there, or loved ones who will meet us when we cross over? Does Saint Peter guard the pearly gates or are we written into the book of life at Yom Kippur? I don't know, I don't think anyone really knows. But we all believe there is something—and that is called faith.

I don't know where Andrew--or his soul—is, or what he is now, or who he is. But I know he is at peace and he is happy. And that lets me put one foot in front of the other every day.

Who would have thought all three would be gone so soon and so close together. But I have faith they are sitting just like this, together, somewhere, smiling, looking over us all.

FROM ANDREW
June 7, 2014

I am at all of Nicole's games, so proud of her.

I SEE YOU every day.

Often I am right next to you, in the same room with you watching what you are doing. I am so close I can feel your breath, I can see into your eyes. I am there and I watch you work for hours. I am next to your bed at night protecting you, and I watch Nicole at night and make sure she is safe. I travel around and watch over Greg and Todd, and Katie, and Wally and Matt. I was so proud of Katie and Todd at their graduations—I was sorry they could not see me, but I walked down the aisle with them and stood behind them with my hand on their shoulders when they received

their diplomas. I was standing there so proud when Nicole dressed in her college jersey for the first time and stepped on the ice and in the net the first time. She could not see me, but I know she knew I was there cheering her on like so many other times. I stand outside Mommy's office every day at work and see how hard she works and admire how smart she is and how much she has accomplished—I should have told her this more when she could hear me.

I miss everyone so much—as much as you miss me. But I try to say hello once in a while. I will play with your GPS, or the lights, or move your computer screen around when I can—I am still learning how to do that so be patient with me. When I get lucky I come visit you in your dreams, like before Nicole's games or on Mother's Day. I might blow out a candle one day, or come to you as a butterfly. I try to communicate in so many ways, but you can always sense me near you. You can't see me, but you can feel me, you can feel my love, you can feel my compassion—and that is all that I am now.

I am trying to help Jovi. I know how lost she is and how she feels so alone. She knows how much I loved her and how much she loved me. I appreciate all that Dad is doing to help

her, and hopefully she will find someone to love one day and live a long happy life. I look down at my left hand and see the wedding bands we got each other and it reminds me of her love. It reminds me of our unconditional love for each other. Thank you for giving me that to have with me forever.

There is so much love now around me, all the people I knew before. All the people I missed so much and I cried over—Poppy and Uncle Cy and Aunt Flo and Uncle Herb, and so many more. There are also those I never met before but I knew so much about—like Grandpa Gary. They talk to me all the time and tell me how wonderful  a life they had, and how blessed I was to have had such a full life. Although it lasted only a short time, it was amazingly full of love, experiences, and challenges. As Daddy has said so many times since I left you—I lived more in my twenty-one years than most people live in a lifetime. When I do relax here, I lay my head on Daisy, and cuddle with Louie and Punky. Daisy runs around pain free, she has no arthritis here, and jumps up and down with excitement. She is like a puppy all the time.

I see Daddy in his office every day, and I cry along with him. We had so many plans together, there were so many hopes and dreams that will never be fulfilled. There were so many things Dad was looking to pass along to me—his father's cuff links, his tallis, pictures, stories, and so much more. Now they are in the house with no clear future. I know he will find someone who will take these items one day and keep them as precious and as valuable as he has kept them for years, and as I would have kept them. It might take time but I am sure they will find a home. I know he can't go skiing anymore or SCUBA diving or surfing—those were our activities— our bonding time. But maybe one day he can carry on and go with Nicole and Mommy, or Greg and Todd. One day, I know, he will realize I will be there beside him when he does, not in the doorway blocking him from these things we used to do together.

I miss being called Thor, or Booboo, or even Andrew. I miss

that so much. I miss being hugged and feeling the love. I miss Mommy running up to me and hugging me every morning like she had not seen me for months. I miss the smile on her face. I miss her happiness.

I am also at peace. Like I was when I was a little boy. I have no anxiety, I have no stress, I have no ADD or OCD or anything else, and my kidneys don't hurt me at all. They don't even know what that is here. Uncle Cy and Aunt Flo play golf and they can swing their clubs painlessly, Poppy tends to a garden that never dies and is always watered. He can kneel without pain and work all day, he is so happy in his own garden here.

I carry around some change here too, the beautiful State of Colorado quarters. I put one down on the ground once in a while when I know you are around, or in your car, or in your pocket. Not just for my family, but I know my friends have found these precious coins as well. It brings joy to my face when I see the smile on your face when you pick it up—knowing it came from me.

There are so many things that were left unsaid. And there is no real place or time to start to say them now. I know how much I was loved—I was told it every day. Maybe I should have said it more often, or showed it more often. But I am at peace and you know how much I loved, admired and looked up to you both, Mom and Dad. You know how much I appreciated the cars you bought me and the trips you took me on, and just cooking breakfast and dinner for me each and every day. I did have a wonderful life, and you know that goes without saying.

And as I told Mommy on Mother's Day—I have to go now. Daddy—enjoy Father's Day, read the cards I gave you in the past few years, they mean so much more now—the words I wrote; and keep writing your journal—I read every single word and like so many others I cry at every thought. It is my first Father's Day in

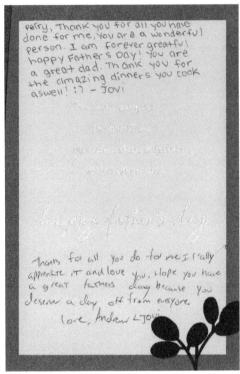

Perry, Thank you for all you have done for me. You are a wonderful person. I am forever greatful! happy Fathers Day! You are a great dad. Thank you for the amazing dinners you cook aswell! :) - Jovi

Thanks for all you do for me I really apprecitate it and love you. Hope you have a great fathers day because you deserve a day off from everyone.
love, Andrew & Jovi

My last Father's Day card to you. I meant every word in it.

heaven and I will be patting Tiger on the head, and hugging him from here.

I love you more now than ever, and I truly know now what love means.

I will write more soon—I promise.

Andrew

NOT ADVICE, BUT JUST OUR CHOICE IN LIFE
June 12, 2014

WE ALL GIVE and take advice from many people throughout our lives, and this is one of those times where I am not giving advice but, rather, talking about a decision Dorothy and I made and continue to make throughout our lives. For some people, this is a relevant discussion, for others, and for other reasons, it might not be.

Andrew's days experimenting with lemons

During our children's lives we tried to provide for them. We struggled to give them good, fun lives. We gave them, or hope we gave them, a good childhood filled with love, memories, and, mostly, whatever they wanted. We took them on a few cruises, they went to summer camps when they wanted to, they had good equipment when they played sports, and we ate out at their favorite restaurants when we could. We tried not to have our children want anything that they could not have, we wanted to provide them with whatever they wanted that was within reason. Thankfully, they were pretty reasonable throughout their childhoods. We tried to teach them the balance between getting what they wanted to live a fun life and, at the same time, being financially responsible in what they wanted.

Was there a cost to this? Of course there was. Sometimes we had to carry a balance on our credit card for a while until we paid it off. Long term, we don't have a lot of funds in our retirement accounts, and will probably have to work longer than we had wanted to. We made a choice, maybe not a one-time choice, but maybe a series of decisions throughout the past twenty-one years that really did become one choice. We put our kids first, and our retirement second. Was it a good choice? Who knows. Let's see how we do in retirement. But in hindsight, and with the way things happened, we are happy with the choices we made.

Andrew experienced so much in his short twenty-one years. He traveled to many places, he became a certified SCUBA diver and went SCUBA diving in many, many places, he went to the college he wanted to and skied in Vail every weekend. He had good hockey equipment, he had a snowboard he loved and was proud of, and he traded going away to camp one summer for a very nice paintball gun he loved to use. I am glad that he had all of this. I know he was happy, and as anyone who knew him knows—he was not material-istic at all. He asked for things, but was always reasonable. He would buy his boxers and T-shirts at Target because they were cheap and fine for him. But he liked to buy his shirts at Abercrombie, because he liked the way he looked in them.

He also knew he was loved. Not because of what we bought him, or where we took him, or what he had, but because he felt it in his heart. He could feel the love. He knew we never missed his hockey games, and, when he was a little boy we never missed his soccer games. Getting to our kids' games and showing them our support was our highest priority. I went to every bar mitzvah and bat mitzvah lesson the kids had, to make sure they knew what they had to know, and to help them when I could. We made it to every school play and every concert they were in. They were, and still are, our lives.

So what am I saying to people? That depends. There are plenty of people who read my posts and have a hard time making rent every month, and maybe take a short vacation every year to the shore. Others who read my posts have all the money they ever will need or want, and their children never know from want or need, and are provided with vacations, toys, equipment, whatever. And then there are those in the middle—like us. Everything we buy we make a choice. Each expense that we pay comes from somewhere, and it usually has to come out of somewhere else. If you work late every night and don't see your kids too much during the week, that is fine, it is your choice. But then don't be upset when they grow up and you are not as close with them as you would like to be. Sort of Cats in the Cradle situation. Maybe you can provide for them financially, and at age ten they have their college completely funded, but did you watch them play soccer on the weekends and take them out to dinner just to talk? How many of us have heard stories of parents who worked themselves to death in well-paying jobs, only to leave their families with lots of money—but only one parent.

Don't miss your kids growing up. Don't miss out on the most joyous things you will ever see—your kids in a concert in third grade, your son making his first score in soccer or hockey, your daughter's first recital, whatever is important to them. These things will never be re-lived, and trust me, your kids will remember that you were there throughout their lives—and they will appreciate it.

For us, maybe we won't have enough to retire when we want to. Maybe we will have to work a few more years, maybe we didn't get a fine piece of jewelry or a nice watch when we traveled. But we were happy making sure our children had what they wanted, and we taught them the value of a dollar along the way, as well as the value of their parent's love.

Andrew showed me some tie-dye shirts he bought when he was in Boulder, and to my surprise he told me he bought them at the Goodwill store. He went there while he was doing his laundry in town. He also had several knick-knacks in his apartment from a place called The Box in Boulder. It is a place where people donate stuff, just drop it off, and others come and take what is there. No charges, no records, just a nice place to exchange items. We brought a lot of Andrew's items there because he learned about charity from giving the stuff he didn't use anymore to The Box—some pictures, old electronics, speakers, clothes—he donated a lot while in Boulder. Andrew was a very compassionate person, and he always gave a homeless person a dollar, or the change in his pocket. It was important to him to make a difference in someone else's life.

Is this advice? I hope not. I am not preaching, I am not telling you how to live your life or how to save your money. What I am just saying is to look at your priorities. If your retirement means that much to you and you want to stop working at sixty, that is fine. If you can't see your children's soccer game because you have to work Saturday or lose your job, that is fine, it's a choice you don't have. But let's face it—our kids are our lives for most of us, make sure they know it. I know deep in my heart that both Andrew and Nicole know they are our first and only priority in life.

I hope I don't offend anyone with this entry, but this topic has come up in so many conversations over the past months that I just felt I wanted to write about it and express my feelings. If your viewpoint is different, I do understand. If you do not to have children, by choice or not, I hope you are not bothered by this post, but maybe you can take something else away with you. The opinions stated in this entry are just mine.

HAPPY FATHER'S DAY, MY SON
June 18, 2014

THIS IS A hard post to write. Not because I am tearing, or because it is overly emotional. It is because I don't know how to start it or how to put it. I guess the best way it to say it right from the start.

I am going to meet my grandson for the first time this weekend. Andrew's and Jovi's son. He is about eighteen months old and it is the first time I will see him. Dorothy was there for the birth, and Andrew and Jovi spent time with him last spring, but this is the first time I will see him.

Now for the backstory.

A little over two years ago, after they had been living together for a while, Jovi got pregnant. The two of them spent that summer in our home here in New York, but Jovi did not know what to do and so they waited until they returned to Boulder to take the test and it came back positive. After some thought and conversations they decided to keep the baby to full term and put the baby up for adoption at birth. They called Dorothy and me, and we fully supported their decision. They knew, as did we, that they were too young to keep the baby and that Dorothy and I were too old to start again with a new baby. They wanted this baby to have a wonderful and fulfilling life and the best way for that to happen was to let go of him (yes, it is a him) to a loving family who would raise him as their own. For those of you who don't know, Jovi was adopted herself.

The next several months were pretty amazing. We traveled to Boulder every other week to take Jovi to the doctor, to meet with adoption agencies, to sign papers with them, and to make sure everything was going well. They learned about and decided on an open adoption, which meant that they would be a limited part of the baby's life, seeing him once a year, getting pictures of him regularly, and knowing how he was doing. It was pretty amazing to see this young couple mature so much and make all of these decisions and be so responsible. Dorothy and I were there to help them, but, make no mistake, they decided on the family themselves, they went to court to sign the papers, and they did everything. We were standing behind them, offering them advice and supporting them the whole time, but it was their process.

The family. One decision they made was that they were eventually going to return to New York and they wanted to be close to him, so they chose a New York agency to lead the placement. They looked over dozens of very detailed family profiles and had to make the hardest decision of their lives—who were they going to give their own flesh and blood over to. Andrew wanted the baby to be the first child that this couple had, he wanted it to be special in that way. Jovi wanted a family that traveled and saw the world—something she was never able to do but wanted her baby to have the chance for. They wanted a family, they said, that would spend time with the baby, rather than a family that presented itself as wealthy and said, "the baby would always be taken care of." They did eventually choose a family from Long Island—far enough away that they would not be tempted to go watch him from afar, but close enough that they could feel him nearby.

They first did a Skype session with the potential parents. I met the couple at the office before the Skype session, then they met Andrew and Jovi, and that went so perfectly. They are warm and loving and we could all sense that. Then the couple went out to Boulder to meet them later on, which also went well. Andrew called us. He was so happy to meet them, and his intuition told him how loving they were and how grateful his son would be to be raised by such wonderful people.

The baby was born in January last year, a few weeks early, happy and healthy. Dorothy arrived in Boulder a couple of hours after the birth and spent a week or so with the three of them for moral and physical support. We have many pictures of all of them with the baby. The day that Dorothy left for home, the adopting family arrived and spent several days with Jovi and Andrew in the hospital. Because the baby was small, and because it was an adoption, he spent a couple of weeks in the hospital. They did not want him to be alone, so Jovi was kept in the hospital as well.

People ask us if I went out there when the baby was born. No, I did not, and could not. I could not handle it and we all knew it. I had spent way too much time with them during the process and was an emotional wreck at that point. If I had gone out there and seen the baby, held the baby, looked into his eyes, who knew what would have happened. So we all made the decision for Dorothy to go on her own at that point.

It was a very hard day for them when they left the hospital— alone. No matter how much you prepare for it, no matter how much you know you are doing the best thing for the baby, no matter what—it hurt them so much letting go. The baby stayed in Boulder another couple of weeks for legal reasons, and they spent time with him during those days. They called every night and told us how wonderful the couple was and how the baby was growing and eating and smiling.

They knew they made the right choice.

Andrew went back to studying, he was just in the middle of his junior year. Jovi slowly went back to working. Every month they received pictures of the baby and exchanged e-mails with the parents. We cherish those pictures. They both had their son as their screen savers, background images, keychain pictures, and on the wall next to their bed. As Dorothy and I do now.

What gives us great peace is that Andrew and Jovi went to see the baby when they were here in New York. They came home gleaming and bragging about their son. That visit made their spring. The picture we love the most these days is the one of Andrew holding his son. Now it is time for me to hold his son, for a few minutes.

We keep in touch with the parents, they still send pictures, we exchange e-mails, they even came to Andrew's funeral—which meant more to us than anyone could imagine. They have pictures of Andrew

Andrew was so proud that they changed the lives of a couple who could not have their own child

as a young boy and as a young man, as well. We have been writing letters to the baby and talking about Andrew and Jovi so that when he grows up he knows them through our words.

We have told people in person about the baby when we see them. Andrew's friends tell us that he talked about his son a lot, with pride and honor gleaming from his bright face. Now it is time for me to meet my grandson for the first time. Nicole is going with us, she is excited to meet her nephew for the first time. There is so much more I want to say, and need to say, but I am going to keep that for later. I want to talk about how we feel, about the fact that a part of Andrew is still alive and how blessed we are to have him around. But more to come soon.

I hope you are as happy as we are about this. We are at a loss many times with our feelings, so happy at times when we look at the pictures, and yet so sad that Andrew is gone.

Happy Father's Day, my son. You're the first one in heaven. Your son will miss you his entire life.

DEAR ANDREW, I MET YOUR SON
June 22, 2014

DEAR ANDREW,

I had an amazing day yesterday. I met your son for the first time. Mommy, Nicole, and I took a ride to Long Island and we met our grandson, and Nicole met what will be her only nephew.

Your son is gorgeous. I want you to know that, but I am sure you already know that. He is playful, adventurous, funny, and so happy. He smiled the entire time we were with him. He reminds us of you when you were a little boy. He has beautiful red hair, just like you used to have. He has wide round eyes—just like Jovi's. He has your walk and your quick feet, and he is small and petite like Jovi. He is the perfect mix of the two of you.

We brought him a few things, from all of us. First, we brought him a stuffed giraffe, just like you guys gave him last year and when he was born. He immediately took and played with it, and of course shoved it into his mouth. And after a few minutes he threw it down and went on to the next toy. But he kept on going back to it, kept on picking it up and playing with it. Little does he know the link between that little stuffed animal and his parents. We will keep giving him a giraffe every year when we see him, as long as we can, and one day he will wonder why, and he will read the letters I am writing him and realize it was the first and only toy his mom and dad gave him when he was just a few days old. We also gave him a hockey stick. Not just any stick, but one of those we gave out at your Bar Mitzvah. He grabbed the middle of it, but Nicole quickly corrected him and taught him to hold the right end of the stick—maybe her lesson will "take." There were also a couple of small foam pucks for him to hit around. He didn't know what to do with them yet, but I am sure he will learn soon.

Nicole took to him so well. She picked him up and held him—and she smiled—and I cried inside. She took pictures of herself holding Tiger, as he is called, and insisted that I take more of them, as well, with her phone. This way she will forever have them with her. People call him Tiger because of his gorgeous red hair, just like you. Jovi and the nurses called him Tiger in the hospital when he was born—it stuck.

I held him. I held him like I had held you so many years ago. I was proud of him, and loved him so much, although I have known him for only a few minutes. He is part of me, he is part of you. He is the part of you that is still here on this planet and will forever be here.

I looked around, and I did not see you. But I know that you were there. I know that you are always there with him. I know that you will forever watch over your son, protecting him, showering him with love from heaven, and being his guardian angel throughout his life. You will protect him and help him make tough decisions, just like your father did for you, for as long as I was allowed to. He will one day want to know more about you, and in the letters that Mommy, Jovi, and I are writing him he will know you, we hope, as well as if you were still here holding his hand. That is our job now, to leave your legacy to your son so that he knows where he came from, and, as we also hope, to guide him in some small way to where he might want to go.

Will he be a reader or a writer? An athlete, or, as Nicole says, an N.A.R.P. (a Non-Athletic Regular Person)? Will he want to know all about you and one day question us about everything you were, or will he just read the letters we write and be happy? Who knows. But no matter what—he is your son, and he will always be your son. His parents tell us he loves puzzles, and loves solving things. We immediately thought of your Rubik's Cubes. He has so much of you in him.

We were with his parents, and the way their faces lit up when they held him was amazing. The words they used to describe their son just filled our hearts with warmth and love. The love they have for him is immeasurable, just like your love for your son when you met and held him. They are amazing parents you and Jovi chose— you guys did a great job.

I am home now. I am also at a different place in life than I was a few days ago. For the first time I held my grandson, I looked into his eyes, and knew he was loved, and when I looked into his eyes, I saw you looking back at me. I see you, and although you are not here with us, you left this world an amazing gift. This world, as well as Tiger's home, is a better place for you having been here for your short number of years. You gave life and happiness to a family that could not have it without your love and your baby. You and Jovi did something so incredibly generous and without any hesitation or regret. Heaven has a special place for you.

I hope that you can one day visit Tiger, and for him to know his father came to see him. It might be a dream, or a butterfly, or a found coin on the floor, but I know that he will love you as you love him and as we love you. I am sure you will see him graduate from kindergarten one day, then from high school and college, and you will be as proud of him as his parents are.

Love never dies, only people do.

WHO'S AFRAID OF GHOSTS
June 27, 2014

WHO'S AFRAID OF ghosts? I remember just a short time ago I used to not walk out in the pitch black. I would look over my shoulder in the dark all too often. When looking in a mirror I would not look to the far edges for fear as to what I would see there—what eyes would look back at me. I didn't want to sit alone on a chair in the dark backyard. When I walked up the stairs from a dark basement I would walk just a tad faster toward the end in fear of that ever-present fearsome ghost grabbing me. Maybe these were normal fears, or maybe conjured up by the fear of the unknown.

But now that has all changed.

I embrace sitting alone for long stretches in the pitch-black backyard. When I look in a mirror, I look to the edges, I look to the farthest point of reflection I can see, I stare at the little shards of a shattered mirror. I sit in the dark often, I stand on the deck at night alone looking at the chairs on the patio below me. When I get home late at night I sit in my still car alone for just a few more moments than usual. I walk slowly from the car to the front door. I am no longer afraid.

And I am sure I am not alone. I am sure every grieving parent knows why I do this.

I look at that chair and wait and wish to see Andrew there staring back at me and smiling. I recall the hours he and I spent during his last summer, sitting in those chairs talking and listening by the fire. I look in the mirror in hopes of seeing my son's face looking back at me for just an instant. I stand on the deck alone  hoping that I will hear his voice saying, "Daddy, I am okay." Just to hear his voice one more time.

I long to be one of those grieving parents who has a conversation with their child who was taken from them way to soon. I want to sit up at night and see him sitting at the end of the bed and I have a conversation with him until he says he has to go—but he tells me he is happy and peaceful and that he wishes for me and Mommy to be happy again. I want to hear him say he will be there waiting for us when our times come. I want to be one of those who sees their child's beautiful face looking back at them in the mirror, or their image standing beside them in the reflection. I want, or, should I say I need, to know that my son is at peace, but I want to hear it from him, or from what he has become.

I long to see the ghost—that ghost that I no longer fear but now embrace.

Perry

IT MUST HURT
July 3, 2014

A CLIENT WAS over a few days ago and we were talking about Andrew and hockey and such. He asked some other questions about Andrew, so I showed  him Andrew's trophies in his bedroom, amongst all of his other treasured belongings. Afterwards, my client said "it must hurt" to go into his room. It made me think.

 Yes, it does hurt to go into his bedroom, to see all of his precious belongings—to see his childhood toys, his guitar that he learned to play on collecting dust, his skateboard that does not bring anyone anywhere anymore. It hurts to see the paintball gun that he loved to use just sitting there, to see his Rubik's Cubes, some solved, others that will never be solved because he is not here anymore. His New York Rangers sticker peeling off the window because he is not there to fix it, right next to his

Harrison Huskies sticker and his Rye Mariners sticker—all parts of his life.

To see the things I gave him that I knew he would like to play with or just to have, like his collection of foreign coins he'd been collecting since he was five. There is also the light cube that one of my dearest clients gave me because he knew Andrew would appreciate it (see it here). Andrew never got to see it because it arrived the day before we lost him—that really hurts because I know he would have stared at it for hours in amazement.

But I also find comfort in his room.

I look at his paintball gun and recall all the good times he had with it. I used to watch him take it apart and meticulously clean it. He used to exchange parts with his friends and use different triggers, and different tanks—he loved to just experiment and try different combinations. I look at the Rubik's Cubes and recall a story Todd tells. Todd handed Andrew the Cube in front of some of his friends, and in the time it took for Todd to ask his friends how long did they think it would take Andrew to solve it, and for them to answer that he would not be able to—Andrew handed the solved Cube back to Todd. Everyone was amazed.

I look at his top shelf full of trophies. Not just hockey, but chess trophies and soccer trophies as well. Lasting reminders of the triumphs Andrew and his teams earned  over the years. I remember each and every one of them. I remember the games, I remember the teams, I remember the embraces afterward. I was fortunate enough to have coached Andrew's teams for nine years, as well as spring leagues and tournament teams. It brings joy to my heart when I think how proud he was to be part of each and every team he was on. He was never the star of the team, but he loved being part of it. We have received so many messages from his teammates telling us how Andrew was such an integral part of their teams, and they usually mention how he made them all smile and laugh—no matter what. Looking at his wall of pucks that he collected over the years… There are so many that we never got to put up.

His electric guitar is also still in his room. I look at it and wonder how it sounded when he played it. He used to not want to bother us so he plugged it into his amp and used his headphones, so we never really heard him play. But his friends said that he played for them, and we hear he was pretty good. He also had an acoustic guitar from Uncle Joe, which his cousin has now. He is learning to play as well, in Andrew's honor—that makes me happy.

I also see Andrew's black and white flannel shirts hanging up, and I hang them on his door knob so I see them every day when I walk down the hall. I see his T-shirts and his team jackets. Although he outgrew many of the clothes he had, he kept them as a reminder to himself of the good times he had when he wore them. There are shirts from our farm visits, from old hockey teams, from school—all too small for him, but memories attached to them. Some of those memories still live on with me, but some of them known only to him and passed along with him. Some of the shirts we will keep forever, but others will be made into memory quilts for those who knew and loved Andrew.

What else is there? He has the license plates from his cars—he loved, loved, loved to drive, and I love the fact that I can see his license plates and remember the smile that he had whenever he drove his Jetta or his RX8. There is an armrest that he took from his high school auditorium. I asked him about that and he said he just thought it was cool to have. He also had some keys to the school, along with a pad of library passes and a pad of late passes—I don't know where he got them or what they were for, but he thought it was too cool to pass them up. That was my son.

So does going into Andrew's room hurt? Of course it does. It hurts like hell and brings tears to my face every time. But his room is full of who Andrew was, what he was, what he loved, what he wanted to be.

It is full of his happy memories, as well as my happy memories of him, full of my joyous times with him and our entire family.

I would not give up my daily visits to my son's room for anything.

THREE TICKETS
July 12, 2014

IT WAS HARD to say three. The cashier asked us how many tickets do we need, and we choked on the word three. Not because we had never asked for three tickets before, but this was different. This was permanent, this was for the rest of our lives. Our family is now three people, not four.

We finally got the words out, purchased the tickets, and my wife Dorothy, our daughter Nicole, and I went into the Atlanta Zoo and had a very nice day. We walked all around and stayed close, the three of us. We gazed at the animals, pet them in the petting zoo, watched the birds and the gorillas and the lions. We talked about the bears, and the three of us watched the pandas eat bamboo. We were all freaked out by the snakes and the lizards, and we stared at the gorillas that stared back at us. It was so nice just to be there. Dorothy and I were happy that Nicole was enjoying the zoo, as she always has. But it was also so hard for us. Andrew always loved the animals and loved the zoo, he should have been there with us. He probably would have been the first to want to leave, his patience doesn't last all day, but he should at least have had the opportunity to ask us when we were leaving. But we did have a very fun day with Nicole. We needed the few hours to just let go and be happy.

Later that day we went to the Coke Experience. Again, three tickets. And the next day was breakfast for three, and three tickets to the Atlanta Braves game. Just saying three makes me sad. That is our new reality. We are no longer four, we are three. There is the same amount of love between us, just shared three ways now, not four, anymore.

I have to look back. I have to look back and smile. We were four. We had so many experiences and memories as four. We did so much, experienced so much, traveled so much—as four. I have to be so grateful that we were able to do all that with Andrew. I have to be thankful that we were four for so long, or just a short twenty-one years. But it was a wonderful time, twenty-one years that I will never forget. Twenty-one years of great memories. I just hope that I can remember those twenty-one years for the rest of my life, and that Nicole will remember her years with Andrew for the rest of her life.

I have to look at the pictures of the four of us and remember how wonderful life was. I know that the four of us were so close, each of us having a different relationship with the others. My relation

ship with Andrew was far different from Dorothy's. Her love for Andrew was a pure mother's love, he could do no wrong, they never argued, he never fought with his mom. When he was frustrated or upset, he loved his mom too much to argue or fight with her, and he would just walk away and say nothing was wrong. We talk about it, and we really cannot remember a time he talked back to her, fought with her, or hurt her feelings. He was a wonderful son to her.

When he wanted to go somewhere and needed company, or wanted to take a ride, there was always Nicole. They went out to dinner together, or even lunch when they were both home. And anytime there was something missing or short in the fridge, they

would both eagerly go shopping for one or two items, and return home with three or four bags of stuff that we absolutely needed. Stuff like Oreo cookies, Miso soup mix, along with plenty of fruit and vegetables. They would even call Grandma and ask her if she needed anything from the store. And of course they would deliver it to her, usually just in time for lunch or dinner—they planned that rather well, usually. Although they lived apart much of the year, they were emotionally so close to each other.

Then there was our relationship. It was probably more complex than the others. The frustration and anxiety he did not let his mom feel or hear, he let me have. We very rarely argued much, or fought, but he knew that I could

take more than Mom, so he did let it out on me more than anyone else. But it didn't bother me, because I knew where it came from and knew it might have been something someone else caused. He knew I could take the hit. We were also closer than the rest. We spent more time together, we traveled more together. We talked so much during the time Jovi was pregnant, and I learned so much about his thoughts and feelings that it really changed our relationship for the better. We also spent hours out in the backyard his last summer talking before the new fire pit. I learned so much about my son in the past few years. He had grown up so much being away at college, I looked forward to watching him become a man, to watching him grow into the person he was becoming. To watch him become a husband and a father, and see if what I taught him really sunk in. To see if my values and morals, at least the good ones, would be passed on to him. I will think about that, and what might have been, for the rest of my life. A relationship between a father and son is like no other.

But now we are three, and I long to see how Nicole will turn out. How will she find happiness in life. I know that she is a strong person, she is strong-willed, and goes after what she wants. She does not sit back and wait for anything. She is much more independent than Andrew was, she asks for help much less and is determined to do it right—no matter what it is.

Yes, we are three now, but we will always really be four.

A LITTLE BIT ABOUT ANDREW
July 19, 2014

I TALK A lot about my feelings, about our loss, about what people say—and don't say—or how they say it. I talk about what is in my head at any given time, but try to make my posts relevant and interesting, not just to those of us who are suffering but, also, to those whose friends are in situations where what I am writing might, I hope, help.

I am off that track today. I feel the need to talk about Andrew. To tell people who did not know him that well, or at all, about him.

Andrew loved to make people smile and laugh

Andrew was always around. But he was also that person who was quiet, in the background, never wanting the spotlight. He was always invited out with his friends and teammates, and he went out with them often but did so while staying almost anonymous in a big group. He was also a funny kid, as anyone who knows him will attest. He would be quiet in a crowd, then all of a sudden blurt out some funny comment and break everyone up, whether in a locker room or at a party. We heard some of the comments he made in his varsity hockey locker room, all told by teammates with smiles on their faces. He did not look for attention, and was very happy just being there, just being part of a group, part of the crowd, part of a team.

He was pretty popular, and everyone knew and loved him. For his memorial hockey game last December, we had an amazing turnout, and we all laughed and cried. People told us stories about Andrew, from school times to hockey to going out at night. It was truly a night to remember for Dorothy, Nicole, and me. Thank you to those who participated. Perhaps this year's game will grow some, and we will keep this one-game-a-year alive for Andrew.

He never wanted to have birthday parties, or even a graduation party, but he was always invited and always going to someone else's party. He never wanted to be the center of attention, but whom-ever he was talking to—he made them feel like they were the most important person on earth at that moment. He never interrupted you, he gave you his undivided attention, and you felt and knew that. We have heard that so many times.

Nicole in Nicole's dress, and later that day Andrew in Nicole's dress, just so people could smile.

Andrew was close with a lot of his friends. After he was gone many of his friends told us that they would talk to him for hours, just the two of them. They would tell Andrew so much more than they told others, the words therapist and shrink came up many times when others talked about him. He would sit and listen to them and they felt comfort in talking to him. He was such a compassionate, caring, and gentle person that no one ever felt threatened by him or by telling him their deepest secrets, their fears, or what was on their mind. And he would listen and nod his head and make eye contact. And then when they were done, Andrew would respond with some pearl of wisdom that made them feel better. I never heard any of these conversations, he never talked to me about this part of his life, but I heard about it from at least a dozen of his friends afterwards. They all had tears in their eyes when they told me about these conversations, and said that they learned so much by having Andrew just listen to them.

Andrew wanted to be a therapist, a healer, a confidante. Even before he graduated from college, or learned his calling, he was doing this, he was helping others. Very rarely does someone find their calling in life so early. Andrew did. He knew he could heal people not just by talking to them but by making them laugh. Even as a little boy, he would make funny faces for the camera, or do funny things to make others laugh—he loved to make others laugh.

One thing that Andrew did was to collect tickets. He liked to look at them and remember the places he had been, the games he had been to, the concerts he laughed at, the mountains he skied. He had collected hundreds of tickets from Ranger games and from Mets and Yankee games. He saw Meatloaf, The Who (two times), Dane Cook, and Berlin in concert (sitting atop the stage-right speakers: he couldn't hear for a few days after that). He had tickets from the Circle Line, Westminster Dog Show (Exhibitor), NBA Championship games, World Series tickets, and backstage passes. He kept them all in a small wooden box in his room next to his bed.

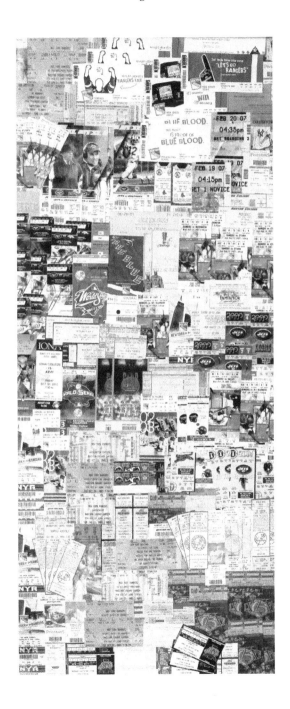

Several years ago, I had heart stent surgery and was unable to do anything for a few weeks. I had an idea that took the better part of that time. I had a board cut five feet tall by two and a half feet wide. I hijacked his ticket box, went downstairs and meticulously sorted the tickets on the floor. Some were sets of two, others were three, and some were fours. I then applied them to the board. No real order, no real pattern, just his memories all laid out on twelve-plus square feet. After I was done, I called him downstairs one evening to show him what I had made for my son. He was amazed, overwhelmed, and truly appreciative of this gift. We had it framed and it has been in his room ever since.

Those who have been to our home have seen the board, he showed it to everyone, and it hangs in his room. It is his memories of his life. It is now our memories of our son. We remember the games now, we remember the concerts we took him to, we remember riding the Circle Line as a family. It is still Andrew's ticket board, but it is now our memories. I often go into his room just to look at it. The box is still there and has so much more in it, maybe one day I will make another board.

We gave Andrew to the world, and we hope the world is a better place for the time he spent here. We hope that those he met, those he befriended, are better people for the time they spent with our son.

THE LAST DECISIONS
July 26, 2014

THEY SAID TO send over a suit and shoes to dress Andrew for the final time. We pulled them out and laid them on his bed and just looked at it. He had a brand new suit that we had just bought, only a few months old. We looked at the suit a good long time. That was not Andrew, this was not the person we raised for twenty-one years. This was not what he was comfortable in. We decided there would be no suit.

Hockey was what Andrew loved. It did not define him, but it  was his passion. He felt free when he had his jersey on and played on the cold ice. He had no worries, no fears, and felt so great to be part of a team. So why would we put him in a suit? Nicole came upstairs with Andrew's Rye Mariners jersey, number 17, and that was it. He would wear his hockey jersey one last time, forever. He would be more comfortable and free in that than anything else.

And shoes? Andrew rarely wore shoes. He hated them. So why put them on him now. He and Wally would spend days without shoes, probably the whole summer if we let him. They went to get pizza one day and they were told that they needed shoes, but since they did not have them the owner of the shop gave them four small pizza boxes to tape to their feet so they would not be barefoot. And they had their pizza and were happy. Unfortunately no one took a picture of that—I would have loved to see that. So how could we put him in shoes now, or even socks.

So Andrew is dressed in his Mariners jersey and a pair of khaki pants. No suit, no shoes. That is the way he would like to be.

Andrew also wore a ring. He wore it like a wedding band on his right ring finger. As far as Andrew and Jovi were concerned, they were, for lack of a better word, married. They were deeply and passionately in love. They lived together for a long time, sharing a small single bed. They had a child together, they ate most of their meals together, and bought each other these cute little token gifts. They were so much in love. The ring came home to us in a small bag along with Andrew's other belongings. How could we leave it in the bag, or in the house? How could we not put it back on his finger for him to wear forever, as I am sure his love for Jovi and their child will last for eternity.

We also needed a tallis for him to wear. The plan was for me to be buried in my Bar Mitzvah tallis, and Andrew to keep his. My father's tallis from Israel, which is the one I wear to temple since my father passed, would stay in the family and be passed down. But that has changed now. I wanted to keep my son's tallis. I did not want to part with it. I want someone else to wear it one day. I did not want it gone for good. So Andrew now wears the tallis I was Bar Mitzvahed in. And his tallis sits in the drawer in my bedroom, still in the tallis bag that he designed and I made, and will one day be given to someone to wear at their Bar Mitvah.

But what else? What else is there we could do?

This past Spring I bought a small Corgi replica car of Andrew's car—a Mazda RX8, black all around. I purchased it so that he could take it back to school and look at it once in a while. My wish was that he would look at it and remember the feeling of freedom, the sense of pride, the feeling of the wind in his air when he drove the car. I wanted him to remember this and maybe it would take a little stress out of his day and bring him some pleasure and relaxation to remember this feeling. He was so happy to have that little toy model--even here in New York.

He left it on his night table and was so happy when he looked at it. So that little toy, that little black model that brought relaxing memories and brought the memory of peaceful driving was there resting next to him forever.

And there was one more thing. Andrew's beloved Daisy.

Daisy was with us for almost fourteen years. She traveled with us, loved us, and we loved her back. Each and every morning when

he was home, Andrew would lay down and hug Daisy and kiss her and talk to her. It was their special time every day. The same was true when he came home from college—he had to spend time with her right away, hugging her, laugh-ing with her, and she would lick his face until he could not take it any longer. Daisy passed away, very quietly and peacefully, a few months before Andrew left us. We had her body cremated and the ashes put in a beautiful flower-covered tin. Over the summer we talked about what to do with her ashes. Should we sprinkle them in the lake that she so loved to swim in? Should we release them into the air from the car that she loved to drive in? We spent weeks over the summer, but we never settled on what to do with her.

A day or so after Andrew passed I was in my home office and I saw the tin with what remained of our beloved Daisy. How could

I leave her on the shelf in my office, alone? How could I let my Andrew be alone forever? So the last thing I did was to place Daisy in Andrew's arms. They would be together forever. Daisy would be right there with Andrew forever. Alongside him when they entered their eternal peace. I am sure they are together today, and will be forever, bringing a smile to Andrew's face, and a wag to Daisy's tail.

There we stood, looking at our son for the very last time. We would never see his beautiful, smiling face again. This was it. But in that moment when we looked at him, he was at peace. There was no stress or anxiety in his face. There was nothing hurting him or bothering him, there was no pain. And we said that to each other. We found some peace in that, Andrew was at peace.

There he was in his Rye Mariners jersey, with Daisy in his arms, his car neatly parked next to him, wearing the ring that tied him to the woman and child he loved so much, wearing my Bar Mitzvah tallis—and he was at peace.

Then I had to do the hardest thing I will ever have to do. We motioned for the director to close his eternal resting place. And I watched as I gazed upon my son's beautiful face for the last time. We never turned away, we just backed up and sat there in the first row as people came to greet us and pay their respects. And we were numb.

ANDREW'S FOUNDATION
August 1, 2014

This is what being on a team feels like

HOCKEY, SOCCER, BASEBALL, softball, lacrosse. Our kids played some or all of these sports growing up. We think back on all of the good times we had during those seasons. They made great friends, learned amazing life lessons, learned to be a team player. They benefited in so many ways—not just in making each of them a good teammate but, also, a better person, a more compassionate person, and a better human being. They made friends that will last them through school and beyond. The memories, the jerseys, the trophies all become part of their lives and who they are. No matter how the teams did, they learned, they enjoyed, they grew.

Aren't we all proud of the fact that we were able to afford these sports for our kids. Some were less expensive than others, some were too much, but we knew the value of being on a team and we stretched our dollars. We woke up early to take them, stayed out late for practices, and took off Fridays to go to tournaments. Their teams became our lives for years and we were very happy that way. The other team parents were our closest friends for the season and beyond. We wore their team colors, had team blankets, and cheered and took pictures that we shared proudly with our families.

And then there are the others. Let's talk about them. Those kids who cannot afford to play travel sports. Those kids who, because of family circumstances, cannot enjoy the benefits of being a team player. Of course they can still have success in life, and they do just fine, but they miss out on a huge part of growing up. Thank fully, almost every

Look at the faces of these kids. Everyone is smiling and happy to be part of the team.

organization has a scholarship program that enables these kids to be able to play. They can benefit from being on a team. The organizations realize that those who can afford to play have to support those who cannot afford it—and this is a good thing. I have seen several scholarship players become such an integral part of the team and learn so much. Andrew also saw this, and it meant a lot to him.

So there is money and a spot for those who cannot afford travel sports. What still is missing, however, is a big part of participating in sports. And Andrew realized this. Let me tell you a story.

One of Andrew's hockey teammates would tie a pair of hockey socks around his shoulders to give the appearance that he wore shoulder pads. Without them he could not play, but he could not afford to buy real shoulder pads. His family just did not have the extra money to spend. Andrew talked to me about this and he did something about it. We went to some Manhattanville Men's Hockey players we knew and told them about this player, and they were more than glad to donate a pair of pads for him. They knew the value of being on a team and wanted to help. Another player had holes in her gloves and we arranged for new gloves from the Woman's team. And yet another player had such large feet that most hockey stores did not stock his size, but someone on Manhattanville was glad to donate his used, but very large, skates. Andrew was touched by this and really worked to get used equipment to players in need.

The point of the story is this. While most organizations have scholarship money for spots on a team, and most school teams don't charge for playing or can subsidize players, there is nothing for those players in need of equipment. Organization won't buy new skates for a player who wears out or outgrows skates. If a player's stick breaks, there is no replacement that someone is going to give her. If a kid is using an expired helmet (yes, they do expire these days), no one is there to purchase him a new helmet so he can continue to be part of that team.

This is where we want to come in. The friends, teammates, and family who loved Andrew. The clients, peers, friends and, co-workers of his parents.

In Andrew's memory, and in his honor, we are stepping in and helping these kids who need equipment but who cannot afford what they need. We will be there to buy them a new helmet, a new stick, shoulder pads, or even socks. We are going to make them whole again so that they can continue to pursue their dreams. This is going to be a gift, not a loaner, not a rental, but a gift that they get to keep as their own. We are not going to make a public statement about it—we are not going to list who got what, privacy is so important in situations like this. But at the end of the season, or once a year, we will publish a list of what was given out, what items we gifted to needy individuals.

Each and every one of Andrew's coaches had a positive influence in his life. They were all part of his hockey family.

The goal is to make a difference in these kids' lives. We are going to start with ice hockey because that was Andrew's passion. And we want to start out small and learn how to do this correctly. Then our hopes and plans are to expand to other sports as time and finances allow us to.

Just think about how your kids, nephews, nieces, or your neighbors benefited from sports. Think of the fun, life experiences, and other benefits that they were afforded being on a team—and being well-equipped. Look at any ice rink or ballpark and you can see the fun these kids are having and the lessons they are learning in life. Please help us in helping the small percentage of kids who need our help. Let's not lock them out because they could not buy a new stick or new skates. Let our compassion help these kids grow into fine human beings. It's only a small part of their lives, but isn't it worth it?

We do not have a name for the foundation yet but are hoping some creative friend will come up with a great name for us to use. Something that includes his name as well as the idea of what we are trying to accomplish here.

We are not soliciting donations now, but will within a few weeks. When we do, we really hope that we have can have a response that would make Andrew proud of what he started.

MISSING SOMEONE
August 9, 2014

TAKE CARE, see you later, miss you …

We've all said them, we've all heard them. But what do they really mean? Are they merely words? Do we really mean them when we say them, or are they a courtesy when we talk to one another? Some expressions are just that—just expressions for the end of a meeting, the end of a visit, just words at the end of a letter. Take care. See you later. Pretty simple, not much meaning behind them, and not much thought.

But "miss you," that's all the difference. When you talk to someone you have not talked to in a while, you say it. When you

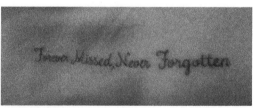

A beautiful tattoo in memory and in honor of Andrew

see someone again, you say it. When you write someone an e-mail or a text, you use it all the time. But do you really "miss" them that much? Or at all? You know you are going to see them again. Maybe in a day, maybe a week, maybe next vacation, but they will be there, and you'll see them again.

But when someone is no longer there, or no longer here, then you learn what the words missing someone really means. Dorothy told me a while ago, through her tears, that she really, really misses Andrew. I thought about it, and so do I. She said that she really learned what the word means now that he is gone, and that missing feeling will go on forever. I guess that is the difference. You can miss someone, but you know they are around. You know you will see them again, you know you can always reach out and touch them.

We can't. Any grieving parent can't. Any child who lost a parent that they were close to—can't. That is really what missing is. That, to us, defines missing someone. That type of missing hurts, it goes down to the soul, it affects you profoundly. Some days that missing consumes us, and we have a hard time getting around it, we have a hard time functioning. Other days we feel it, but we cherish the time before and we smile.

You know you can no longer hug your parent, or your friend. You can't call your brother or sister to tell them something funny happened to you. You can't say something to them that you always wanted to tell them. You can't reach out to them for advice, as you always did before. That is missing someone. That redefines what it means to miss someone. I had a conversation with a close friend of mine about this. His father passed away a few months ago, and for the first time in his life, he misses someone, truly misses someone. It does not matter how close you were to a person who is gone, just knowing that they are gone, forever, makes missing them all too real. It is no longer just a word.

My father. I miss him every day of my life.

I miss my father deeply. It has been thirty-five years, and not a day goes by that I don't think about him. I have his pictures up in my office and on my desk, I look at them every single day—as I am sure most people who have lost a parent do. What would he have been like when he got older? I wonder about his relationship with my children, would he have spoiled them? I wonder how different I would have turned out had I had a father to ask advice from, and to look up to for the past two-thirds of my life. I missed him at my high school graduation. I missed telling him when I got my first job, and my first promotion, or started my own business. And most of all, I missed him at my wedding and the birth of my children—he should have been there. I miss him. I have learned to live with missing my father. It took most of my life to adjust, but I have. I know that fathers pass before their children, and I look around and see my friends' fathers passing, and I feel so sorry for them, for they will unfortunately learn what missing someone means. And many of them I will miss as well.

I talk to my friends and acquaintances whose parents are passing, for they know that I have lived through it and survived. I can talk to them from experience, and tell them what has gotten me through my life. And hopefully they can find some solace from what I say.

Then there is a different kind of missing. That of a parent missing a child. That is entirely different.

We miss Andrew deeply, down to our souls. The pain of missing him hurts us, not just emotionally, but physically—like a hole in our hearts. But that is a dif-ferent miss. We miss hugging him every day, and seeing him for breakfast. We miss him being our son, calling us for advice, calling us to say hello, just being here. And it won't get better, ever. We missed him this past spring when he should have graduated from college. We will miss him on every trip we take, and know he should have been there. We will miss him when someone gets married in the family, or when someone passes: he should have been there. We went to Dorothy's cousin's engagement party last month, and although we had a very nice time, it hurt knowing Andrew should have been there. He would have enjoyed the food, spending time with Grandma, and listening to the flowing water of a nearby waterfall—he was missed by many. When we grow old we will miss him. Whatever we do, we miss him.

My great-aunt never let us say "goodbye." She would always correct us to say, "see you later."

I miss her a lot. I wonder what she thinks of the expression "miss you."

This journal is dedicated to all those I miss.

LET'S TALK ABOUT ANDREW
August 15, 2014

LET'S TALK ABOUT Andrew, please. Don't be shy, don't be reserved, don't worry about hurting our feelings or making us sad.

Please talk about Andrew. We know he is gone, we know that we have lost our son. We know that G-d has taken our child. Talking about him will not remind us of this, we have not forgotten about it, we never will. It is in the forefront of our minds and the most dominant thought we have every day. It is the first thing we think about when we rise in the morning, and it is what we cry about as we fall asleep every night.

Andrew putting Nicole's Halloween make up on, which made for a great story of how they loved each other.

So let's hear your stories about Andrew. Share with us your memories. Show us you remember him, you cared about him, you knew him. Let us know he is not forgotten. Talk to us like he is still with us, for he is with us, still. Share with us a story we never heard, share with us memories of when he was at your home and did something funny, or when he was with your son and they did something special. I am sure there is a lot about him that we have not yet heard.

And not just for us. If you have a friend who has lost a child, a sibling, a parent, a friend—talk about them. Don't shut down. Don't change the subject. Don't think other things are more important. There is nothing more important to a grieving person than to know

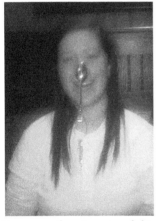

you care. There is nothing better to a grieving person than to hear memories of their lost one. Grieving is not forgetting or holding it in, grieving is sharing and caring.

I know it might be hard for you to do this, but is it any harder than me living without my son? Than a young man who just lost his dad? Than a child losing their sibling? The comfort of you taking the time and thought to talk about our lost ones means so much to us that you will never know. But you one day will know, unfortunately. Show the

I am sure there is a story behind this picture—I would love to hear it one day.

courage, true courage, that a friend or family member needs. Step up and join us in talking about our lost ones. Even make the first step, tell us a short story about our lost loved one, or even just tell us you miss them too. You will make us happier beyond words and beyond tears.

And yes, we will cry. Yes, you made us cry. But they are tears of happiness, tears of remembrance. These are the tears we need, and we will cry whether you tell us stories or not. But knowing that you are thinking about us, and helping us deal with our grief means so much to us. So fight through your own feelings of being safe, fight back the thoughts of holding a "safe" conversation. That is not what we want and, more important, that is not what we need.

We don't need to talk about the weather, or the latest Hollywood gossip, or the latest celebrity death. We don't care. We really don't. Nobody really cares.

We want to talk about our lost ones. If you are our true friends, our loved ones, you will see through the tears, fight though your fear of hurting us or making us cry. And please, let's talk about Andrew.

This is the story of Andrew's life—put into a quilt for Todd. Snowboarding, Skateboarding, Hockey, SCUBA Diving, and his Bar Mitvah. This was Andrew, forever with Todd.

DEAR JAY
August 22, 2014

A LETTER TO Andrew's son:

Dear Jay,

Yesterday was one of the hardest and worst days of my life. It was the unveiling of your father's headstone.

Although I thought I was prepared for it--for it was just a piece of granite--I really was not. When I saw his name, Andrew J. Grosser, etched permanently in the stone, it really struck me hard. I was thinking that it was just a small religious rite that we all must endure some time in our lives, but usually for a parent or grandparent. But it was so much more than that.

The Rabbi talked about the ceremony of the unveiling of the stone, the meaning of the stone, the ceremony itself, and the Jewish prayers. But it was the personal side of the ceremony that I really heard and which touched me. He said the stone is not just a marker, not just a place to visit. It is really a monument to Andrew, what he lived for, the fact that he was here on this earth and that he touched so many lives. It will forever bear his name and be a monument to his time with us. There were fifty or so people there, which is a lot for an unveiling. That was a testament to who he was, the lives he touched, and that his light will shine on for a long, long time.

The Rabbi did something that was also very interesting. He asked people to go around the gathering and say one or two words about your dad. Just something that they felt when thinking about him, how he touched their lives, something that they think about when they recall Andrew. The things that came out were very touching.

Always smiling
Compassionate
Always gave me a hug
A true friend
Family
Funny
No Bullshit
Loving
Caring
Sensitive
Great love of animals

So we gathered there not to just unveil his headstone, but to pay tribute to him, to say we will always remember him, to make this a monument to who he was to us, versus just a stone with a name and the dates he was physically with us. It will be a place of peace and recollection for many to visit. Many of us walked to the stream behind the plot and looked into the water and listened to the peaceful flowing of the stream. It reminds me of the peace and tranquility of Boulder. I also know that this is what your dad hears every day—the gentle peaceful flowing sound of water.

At the bottom of the stone is the last line, the epitaph. One line, that's it. One simple line to sum up a person's entire life. What can you say in one line that will be there forever, that everyone who passes by the stone will read and understand and appreciate? Andrew's mom and I went through so many choices—too many to list here. Some were about Andrew's love, some about how we will miss him for the rest of our lives, others about his short time on earth and all that he accomplished and experienced. But all that became moot when Nicole said she liked this:

"Your light will shine forever."

That sums it up for us. Your dad's light will shine forever. Through his compassion, his love for others, the way he touched other people's lives, through that light, he will always shine.

Andrew had a little blue bag of small stones that he bought during one of our recent trips to Yankee Candle. He picked each and every one out of a large box of stones. Each stone was carefully selected to be in his collection—he didn't just fill the bag—he selected the stones one by one. He kept the bag in his night table. I talked to him about them sometimes. He said that he knew I collected and appreciated the polished  stones and minerals and that he was going to give them to me one day, or use them to start his own collection, but that he did dump them on his bed sometimes at night and would look at them and appreciate them. Then put them away until the next time. But there is no next time.

I have had that bag in my office since last August. And while I  liked having it here to look at, to look through the stones, to know that each of them touched him, I decided it was time to share them with the world—much like his mother and I shared Andrew with this world, it was time to share his collection. At the funeral, the Rabbi talked about the bag of stones, as I dumped them for the very last time, from the blue bag Andrew had them in into a large clear bag. I told the Rabbi I was going to pass the bag around the gathered group, and that everyone there should look into the bag and find a stone that touched them, much like each stone touched Andrew. And that they should take that stone out of the bag and make it their own. Keep it as a piece of Andrew, forever. Keep it in their hockey bag, or their pocketbook, keep it in their car, or on their desk. Somewhere special. Somewhere where they will see it or feel it once in a while and be reminded of why they have it. There are a few stones left. I am packing them back up in the blue bag and will send the bag to you to have. Now, when you get older and look at it, you will know about the bag of stones, where it came from, and the meaning behind it.

After the unveiling, our friends and family came back to our home. We spent the whole day and into the night talking about Andrew. What started out as one of the hardest and one of the saddest days of our lives ended very nicely surrounded by those who mean so much to us and those who have helped us survive this past year. We are so grateful to each and every one of them.

TODAY
August 24, 2014

I RECALL THIS day last year.

We spoke to Andrew a few times during the day. His hand was hurting him, for he had broken it on Friday and had it set on Saturday. He was going to get some books today for school, then relax for the day. School started tomorrow.

He was looking forward to starting his senior year—his last year of school. He had worked so hard for the past three years and he was glad to be finishing up. Although he knew he probably needed his master's degree, he was about to complete college. Graduating was something he was looking forward to so much. We talked to him taking just the four classes, a little less stress for him, a little easier—and then completing his degree over the summer with a couple of electives. He was happy that we were not pushing him to finish in May but, rather, suggesting the summer.

We talked about his job. He had a full-time, permanent job with a software company in Denver starting when he graduated. It was his dream job, making great money, living in Boulder, easy hours, and he got it before he even started his senior year. That took so much pressure off him.

We talked about Jovi. She was with her mom for the weekend and he missed her—although she was gone for only a few days. He was very happy with her, and we know that they loved each other unconditionally. He loved her youthfulness and the fact that she

accepted him for whatever he was. He loved to buy her little gifts—like candles, or Hello Kitty notebooks and bags. Whatever he bought her, she was so happy with. And she would bring him food when he was studying, and they would hang out and hold hands for a little while until he had to go back. It was their special time together.

He asked about Buttercup—our new cat. We got her a week

before he got home from college in June and he spent a lot of time with her over the summer, along with Daphne. He hinted at getting a cat out there for the two of them, for his apartment allowed them, but he wasn't sure the two of them could care for one—they were not that responsible.

He reminded me to drive his car every few weeks to keep it in working order and make sure it didn't freeze up. But I had to drive it slowly and had to be careful—I wasn't allowed to drive it like he enjoyed driving his little sports car. The fact is I could barely fit into the car so performance driving it was pretty much not an option.

We talked about some other stuff as well, but it seemed insignificant. When I was there just two days earlier, we had bought some sushi salmon for dinner. He had made some white rice, cut up the fish, made his own rolls. He used the little soy sauce bowls we had bought last week. He was very particular about his soy sauce. He liked a couple of brands and would use only them. He told us that he was going to eat dinner now, then relax, watch some TV, and head off to bed. He would talk to us Monday and tell us how school went on the first day.

We were so happy that he was happy. We were happy that he was in such a good place mentally and emotionally. Everything was good.

Then he went to sleep.

Forever.

There was so much more for him to do, but it was not to be.

There was so much for him to experience, but he never would.

There was so much more for him to tell the world, but we will never know.

We miss you and love you so much.

Today is going to be so hard.

And I don't want to go to sleep tonight at all.

FOOD
August 30, 2014

FOOD. WHAT A topic. But in so many ways Andrew and Nicole's lives are so defined by food and food-related stories.

Andrew had never had this before, but when he saw it on the IHOP menu the last day I was with him, he wanted to try it. He was quite surprised how steak tastes in pancake batter and deep fried. He was obviously not concerned about the calories or fat.

Country Fried Steak & Eggs*
A golden fried 8 oz. battered beef steak smothered in classic country gravy. Served with two eggs cooked your way, hash browns and two buttermilk pancakes. 10.59

Andrew loved his food. He ate almost anything and everything. Both of my kids grew up at Grandma and Poppy's house, they spent hours and hours in Poppy's garden. They learned to enjoy vegetables grown fresh from the garden, raw, grilled, in a salad, whatever. They loved veggies.

Both of them also loved sushi. We made and ate sushi at home from when they were very young, and they were both pretty accomplished at making their own. Whenever we traveled we liked to make at least one meal a sushi meal. The only issue was Andrew and his soy sauce. He was pretty particular about his soy sauce. I remember I brought home another brand one day and he was not happy. He tasted it and promptly sent me back out for "his" brand. There might be a minor difference in the flavor, but he would always know when we switched them on him.

He was never really into fast food—didn't eat at McD's or BK much, but he did enjoy the local pizza shop.

Nicole loves fast food. When she goaltended for the state championship final game, one of the parents told her if she had a shutout, which was almost impossible in the championship game, the parents would buy her anything she wanted for dinner after the game. Given that incentive, on about forty shots she pulled off a shutout. Her reward? We had to stop the bus with twenty kids and thirty parents at McD's on the way back home, 10 p.m., in a snowstorm, somewhere in Syracuse. The team very graciously let Nicole order first. Her order— "The Dollar Menu." The cashier looked at her and asked her what she wanted. She repeated— "The Dollar Menu." Again, the cashier looked at her and then Nicole made it clear— "The entire Dollar Menu, all twenty-two items." From burgers, to a shake, a sundae, chicken sandwich, fries, etc., the entire Dollar Menu. And to everyone's astonishment she sat on the bus and finished the entire Dollar Menu, courtesy of the team parents. That was a one-time splurge, she does not eat like that now! But she was very happy that bus ride home. Three bags all to herself. While others had a burger or a drink, Nicole was in heaven.

Andrew experimented as well. We ate a few times at my favorite restaurant in Port Chester—Chavin, a small Peruvian restaurant. Andrew had eaten there a couple of times with me and enjoyed it, so when the four of us went for my birthday one year he was happy to go back. There were some steak specialties on the menu, some rice and beans, etc. But after perusing the menu for a few minutes, my son ordered

One of Andrew's favorite meals—nice juicy bone-in steaks with escargots in herb butter. We had this in his honor on the 25th.

the skewered cow heart over French fries and rice. He was always in for experimenting with new food and this was no exception. Although I alone accepted a taste from his plate, he seemed to really enjoy that meal, and said he would re-order it another time. Even when we went to the Korean BBQ, he would always order something new and always wanted to try something different.

From when the kids where babies, Uncle Roy has been coming over at least once or twice a week. Roy and Dorothy, and sometimes I, would help out, would make pretty elaborate meals for the five or six of us (once Roy got married). They would make Italian meals, Greek, Jewish, Mexican—and not the usual meals, but some exotic, different plates. Nicole and Andrew would not want to miss these meals—for although they were very different, the food was always a treat. Sometimes the cooking would take three or four hours on a Saturday or Sunday, and we would finish dinner in an hour—but spending the day with Roy cooking was always fun. Roy even talked about this in his eulogy last year. We all looked forward to these well-planned-out specialty meals.

The first time we had people over to our home last fall was our annual wine dinner. It was a hard day for me to cook so much for so many people, but I know Andrew used to enjoy my cooking, and that was my motivation to continue this annual tradition. Each item on the menu was something that he enjoyed, and I made them the way he liked it. After everyone had gone, Dorothy and I did a toast to Andrew, knowing that we did this dinner in his memory.

Nicole last summer started her own garden, using some of Poppy's seeds and all of Poppy's motivation. Although he has been gone for a few years now, Nicole talks about her namesake all the time, and she is so proud that she is carrying on his tradition of a full garden. Last year we had an abundance of fresh vegetables and gave away over two thousand peppers. The zucchini was the largest we had ever seen, and the tomatoes were abundant. I remember Todd coming over at the end of August and picking several of the cucumbers and eating them right from the garden—he was amazed at the way fresh cucumbers actually tasted. We love Todd, but there were none left for anyone else--but he really enjoyed them and Nicole was very happy about that.

This year the garden is once again flourishing, and I hear that we are in expansion mode for next year, which I am very happy about. It keeps Poppy's memory alive, and makes everyone enjoy the summer just a little bit more.

So this year, for Andrew's anniversary, we decided not to stay home and cry all day alone, or even with friends and family. For Mother's Day, Nicole bought Dorothy tickets to the Greenwich Village Food Tour, and what better tribute to Andrew than taking the day and spending it eating our way around Greenwich Village. We followed our very entertaining tour guide for three hours of culinary treats from Murray's Cheese, to pizza, to rollatini and cannoli. While we had a very special time, just the three of us, we knew Andrew would have enjoyed this as much as we did, and we know that he was there with us every step of the way.

Now we start our second year without Andrew. As Cynthia and Pam and other grieving parents have told us, time is no longer marked by the calendar or the year. Time is marked from when our lives changed. The calendar means so little now, our timeline of life has changed.

What is important is that we have made it through the first year. We did not do this alone, for we could not have made it through the last year by ourselves. We made it through with the love and support of so many people. From our family to our friends, Dorothy's colleagues to my close-knit network of ACT! Certified Consultants worldwide, from our new friends in bereavement groups to my clients and hockey friends. Almost everyone has stepped up, made a call, taken us under their wing, joined us for lunch or dinner, done something to show us how much they love us and want us to survive this terrible tragedy. There is a special blessing for each and every one of you. But more important, you know who you are, and we know who each and every one of you are who have helped us.

Thank you so much. Now on to the second year of our lives, which we hear is harder than the first. So please keep calling, keep coming over, keep joining us for dinner, and keep up with us, we need it now more than ever. And as I have said before, yes, we will cry, and please, cry with us. And we will talk about our Andrew, and please talk about Andrew with us.

WHAT OTHERS SAY …
September 5, 2014

SINCE ANDREW'S PASSING, I have received dozens and dozens of notes, letters, e-mails, IM's, from his friends, teammates, and our family. I have kept all of them and when I have the need to hear about my son, I read and re-read them. It brings me to tears every time I read them, but they are tears of happiness to hear how he was loved by so many and how he helped and changed the lives of so many.

I have put together some of them below to share with you. They are unedited and have come to me over the past year. There are so many more, which I will share sometime soon.

Enjoy …

From A.N.:

Dear Perry—today I had quite the unusual encounter. It started off with Google Earth. I was looking at maps and decided to take a "street view" of Rocky Ridge and nostalgia started to kick in. In particular, this story came to my mind—I remember one day, Andrew and I were practicing our yo-yo skills, when we realized we sucked. Our goal was to beat Max (the German boy up the street) in a yo-yo "sleeping" competition (where the yo-yo keeps spinning, once all the string is drawn, typically when tricks are performed) and Andrew had this great idea—why not put WD-40 on the bearings of our yo-yos so that we could beat Max, and sure enough it worked like a charm, and we became the yo-yo king and queen of the block! Max was stupefied because we all had the same model yo-yo!! But I digress. Anyway, as my work day was coming to an end, we have to chase the chickens around to put them back in their coop. It's always a struggle, and we have to walk pretty far into the woods to go find them. And, this one particular chicken, orange/bass in color, looks me dead in the eye, jumps out of the coop and proceeds down into the woods. I followed him quite some ways, nothing out of the ordinary. But then—and I kid you not Perry, I walk in these woods every day, along with my co-workers—this chicken sits down by a hockey puck in a clearing of tall grass. I've never seen the hockey puck, and I walk that path, every day!!! And oddly enough—my whole day fit together in a strange puzzle of nostalgia. I am so sure that was Andrew somewhere, laughing at our times growing up together ...

Andrew playing shuffleboard with his East Hill Farm family.

From K.N.

Perry, I am so sorry to hear about Andrew. I regret being unable to make it yesterday to the services. He was truly part of my farm family and I have so many fond memories of him.

I remember one year at the farm, when they had those hand sanitizer wipes in the barn, he took a bunch of them for no other reason but to be funny. All week, he kept cracking jokes about them, and with anyone else, those jokes would have gotten old. But with Andrew, it was funny every time.

I remember all the times we went to arts and crafts together. We made lots of bead bracelets and fuse bead crafts. We'd always trade at least one craft every day with each other. And, he would sit there until his was done, even if Todd, Lauren and myself had already finished.

I remember him as someone who got along with everyone. Nothing negative ever seemed to faze him at the farm. He was always so upbeat and positive. Just the way he would enthusiastically get up and say hi to Daisy every single time you walked by with her just showed his true self even more. His sense of humor, his kindness, and light-hearted spirit are qualities I will always remember him for.

I'm so saddened that this kind of tragedy has happened to such an amazing family like yours. You all have touched me with your kindness throughout the years. Andrew will always have a special place in my heart. Sending all my thoughts and love your way.

From another A.N.

Hi Perry, Hope you, Dorothy and Nicolle are doing okay. My Mom was just playing with a Rubik's Cube and it made me think of Andrew. He is the one who showed me the algorithm to complete the cube—of course I couldn't' figure it out but he was a good teacher! I just wanted to share that with you. We think about him every day—he was a good friend. I remember he drove me to school so many times junior year during finals, and senior year before I got a car—he'd see me at the bus stop and tell me to jump in his car. And he would drive barefoot. If you ever need anything from us we're right down the street. Our thoughts and prayers are with you all

From B.P.

Andrew really was a great person and one of the friendliest people I have ever met. He has inspired me to live my life to the fullest each and every day.

From L.U.

Andrew was such an amazing person. I went to my first ever music festival with him and my older brother Henry. We camped out for The Gathering of the Vibes in Connecticut for 3 days and it changed my life. I saw how carefree, worldly and full of joy Andrew and all of the other concertgoers were. It changed my taste in music completely and opened my eyes to a world I never thought existed. Andrew will always hold a special place in my heart for this and I am so thankful to have met him and created such amazing memories with him and my brother. I miss him so much

From B.G.

Hi Perry, I just now found out about Andrew—Absolutely shocking. I was definitely one of the few people who really got to know him being that we were roommates for the better part of two years. Those years were really special to me; Andrew had a certain aura to him that was truly unique, truly profound. He had such a light that emitted from his smile, such a positive glow that was unmistakable. You could instantly feel the atmosphere of a room brighten whenever he walked in—the kid was special.

I spent so many days and nights philosophizing with him about everything from consciousness to politics to the value of being a good person, and everything in between. He always had something new to offer to the conversation that changed my perspective; I learned so much through and with him. Every once in a while, I find myself laughing in reminiscence about things we talked about, the witty comments he would make, the way that he could turn anything into a smile.

I just want you to know that when it comes down to it, Andrew, specifically, has positively influenced my life, and he lives on in my own life in how his presence has affected me. I will always look back fondly on my time spent with Andrew, and how I've grown through his being a good person.

He was so smart—everything he came into contact with was left with a residual glow that was simply beautiful. My heart hurts for you and your family, especially because he was all the way out here when it happened. I just want to reassure you that his time spent out here really was a blessing to many people, and that in my experience with him, he made me smile more times than anyone else I've met out here. If there is anything I can do to help you or your family to ease this process of transition, please do not even hesitate to ask. I am going to get together with some people from the dorms in his honor—one last hoorah for the beauty that was Andrew's life.

From A.D.

I didn't want to send this message too soon so I thought that now would be a better time. I wanted to tell you how sorry I am for your loss. I understand that there is nothing anyone could ever do to make the pain go away but I wanted to tell you how much I loved spending summers at EHF with Andrew and Nicole.

He was always smiling when he played hockey—
he loved to be part of the team.

The best memory I have of Andrew is when Nicole and I decided to wake up really early on the LAST day you guys were at the farm and DUMP cold water on him. I just remember how after we dumped this water and woke him up he was NOT upset and was just laughing! (Nicole and I were hysterical) It's a memory that is just so simple but stays with you for a long time. Both your kids are outstanding and hilarious and KIND people and I am so happy that I was able to meet Andrew and your family and shared wonderful memories. I am thinking of you during this difficult time, always.

This was pretty typical at our home during hockey season. Nicole would hang out with everyone until they all fell asleep. Daisy would never want to be left out.

From A.B.

You raised a great kid. I'm thankful every day I got the chance to meet and be friends with such a wonderful individual. Andrew truly touched the hearts of so many people. Thank you for doing such a good job with him. He gave nothing but respect since day one.

And, finally, from M.J.

I'll always remember our last conversation. I dropped you off at your house just hours before you left for the airport to fly to Colorado. Although I wish every day that we could talk just one more time, and of all the conversations we had, I know our last conversation was the perfect one because it reminded me of the great, selfless friend that you are. I use the word "are" because the things you told me are still with me and always will be. It has been a sad day, undoubtedly, but it is the happy memories of you that carry us through days like these. Thank you for everything and I love you brother.

TOP TEN LIST—FROM ALL GRIEVING PARENTS
September 12, 2014

TO ALL OF our friends, family, relatives, co-workers, peers, distinguished alumni:

We know you mean to say something meaningful, sympathetic, and intended to ease our grief and pain. We know you are reaching out to us in our time of need. We know you are trying to be our friend and our comfort.

In our bereavement groups we talk about what our friends and family say to us. And as nicely as I can put this, for all the grieving parents, please think before you speak. Think about what you are really saying. Think about the real meaning of your words. Think about it for a moment before you say it.

This is not a rant, or a bitching session, or letting off steam. This is one of the many topics we discuss in our bereavement parents' meetings, and sometimes it hurts. We are strong enough not to respond to these phrases the way we would like to, but weak in that they really do hurt us. We are strong enough to make it past these conversations, but weak because we cry alone.

This is meant for anyone who is the friend of a bereaved parent. Many, many of us want to say what I am writing here, but don't have the forum to say it—I do. So please, after you read this, and if you relate to it in any way, please share it. Please let others who are much more fortunate than us and have not experienced the grief we carry each day read this as well. You will be doing a great favor to so many people, and maybe sparing a grieving parent the pain of hearing what I am listing below.

Really?
Did someone say that?

1. "I know how you feel." Are you serious? Do you really know what it is to lose a child? Do you know what it is like to lose the most precious thing you have ever held in your arms? Maybe you have lost a mother and/or father, even a sibling. But as we all know, that fails in comparison to the loss of a child. Much of the time, we don't even know how we feel. Between the grief, the crying, the constant struggle to get out of bed every morning, we are at a loss for feelings much of the time. Please, no one really know how we feel but ourselves.

2. "He/She is in a better place now." Really? Do you feel that our children who have been taken from us are in a better place now? Do you think they are better off there than here next to us? And I quote this from another grieving mother— "then tell me which one of your children would like to go to this better place tomorrow and be with my son." I know it sounds a little harsh, but if my son is in a better place now, as some people believe, then is there a child of yours that you would want to join him? There is no better place than right here, right next to me, right in my arms, right here sleeping in his bed every night instead of where he is now.

3. "G-d only gives a person what they can handle." I am not really sure what this means, or is meant to mean when it is said to someone. Most people can "handle" the loss of their child, as most people can handle just about anything. But to think that one person can handle the death of their child better than another, or that G-d makes a

conscious decision that this person is stronger and can handle such a devastating loss is just nuts. We are not "handling" the loss of our children, we are simply living and dealing with it the best we can. When a devastating flood hits a certain region of the country, does G-d do that because those people can "handle" it better? Probably not. And we don't handle it well. We cry, many of us stop working, most of us stop living our lives—that is not handling it. That is surviving.

4. "At least you have other children." So the child that was taken from me was of less value, less love than the children I have left? I should be grateful that I still have my daughter and that minimizes the loss of my son? I know grieving parents who lost one of their three or four children, and they hurt just as much as the parent who lost their only child. You cannot put a value on each child, and when one is taken, the value of the remaining children goes up to compensate for the lost child? It does not work that way, unfortunately. We love each and every one of our children, as everyone does, equally. We treat them the same, we love them the same, we try to make each of their lives unique. When one is taken it is devastating, and it actually hurts the other children that remain behind more than you can imagine.

5. "Everything happens for a reason." Everything happens. Period. Is there a reason why it happens? Probably not. When the father of a family of four dies in a car crash, or the doctor working on a cure for cancer dies, is there a reason? Is the reason that our children died part of some divine plan? How about when someone loses their job and their life is ruined—is there a reason for that? There is no reason my son died—or none that I can accept. It was an accident, and that's it. For someone to say that there was a reason behind it hurts. How would you feel sitting in the hospital with a broken back and someone comes in and tells you that your fall happened for a reason? How would you feel?

6. "You're so strong." No, not really. We are not that strong. We are surviving. That's it. We cry every day, usually more than once. We see our children's rooms and their prized possessions and our knees give out and we lean against the wall for support. We rely on the calls and e-mails and the support of other grieving parents to get us to keep moving forward in our lives. When we smile, we are trying to be happy. When we laugh, which is rare, we are laughing because our children want us to laugh. When we are with others and appear to have a good time with them, we do so because we know our children would want us to have a good time. Then we leave, and cry in the car the whole way home because our children are not here with us.

7. "You make it through the first year—the worst is over." And your basis for knowing this pearl of wisdom is what? You've gone through the loss of a child and have some insight that we do not have, or that other grieving parents do not have? As a matter of fact, the second year is worse than the first—or so we hear from so many in our situation. The one year mark is a milestone. We have had the first Thanksgiving without Andrew. We have had the first New Year's Eve, a night we have always spent together, without our son by our side. We celebrated his birthday last year with our friends and family, but Andrew was not there. And you know something? We are going to celebrate it this year as well. We are going to toast him on New Year's Eve, and we are going to miss him at Passover reading the four questions. All this is in year two, as it was in year one, and it will be just as hard, if not harder. And in year three and four and five. Yeah, we made it through the first year, but the worst is yet to be.

8. "Are you better now?" Actually no. I will never be "better." I will move ahead with my life, I will work when I can, I will one day go out and have a good time—but I will never be better. I lost my son, how can I ever really be better? I might be good one day, the hole

in my heart will be bearable to live with, but it will always be there. I will never be the person I was before I lost Andrew. None of us will ever be better. We have all changed. This goes the same with "are you over your grief now?" No, we are never over our grief. Our children are gone, forever. We will never be over grieving for them.

9. "I didn't want to bring up your son/daughter because I didn't want to remind you of him/her." Please, don't worry about reminding us of our children. They are on our minds from when we wake in the morning with a tear in our eyes to when we fall asleep crying at night. We think about them when we sit at our desks, when we are at breakfast, and when we eat without them at dinnertime. They are always on our minds—more than anything else, ever. What would be nice is if you did talk about our children—if you are comfortable and strong enough to do that, we would like that. It shows us that you care, that you are our friend, that you, too, miss our children. My closest friends talk about Andrew with us all the time, and mostly in the present tense. They help us remember him and remind us that he will never be forgotten by anyone.

10. "I don't deal well with death." Neither do we. We hate the fact that we have to deal with the death of our children, but we have to. We deal with it every day. We know there are many people who don't deal well with death. They will come to the funeral, come sit shiva, go to a wake. But then they disappear because they can't deal with death. Maybe they are afraid that it will affect their children, maybe they are afraid to be uncomfortable during a conversation, I don't know. Some people don't deal well with hospitals and won't visit friends when they are in the hospital, maybe because of infections, or because they can't look at sick or ill people. That is pretty understandable—almost. But not having the ability to overcome your fear of dealing with death to comfort and help a friend who desperately needs it in their time of sorrow? There are still friends of ours to whom we have not spoken much, if at all. Now, a year later,

we are told, it is because they can't deal with death. We're sorry that the death of our child makes you uncomfortable.

"I am sorry for your loss."
A gentle hug.
Kindness.
Friendship.
That is all we seek.

AUTUMN
September 20, 2014

I SIT OUTSIDE in Andrew's garden as the flowers are all dying. I remember planting them just a few short months ago, and watching them grow and flourish, just as I did with my son. I watered them, took care of them, protected them from the elements, and they flourished, as did Andrew. They were beautiful and full for so long, as was he. They gave others peace and comfort when they sat here amongst their beauty.

Now, they are gone. Nothing I could do, nothing I could do to protect them, nothing I could have done to save them. They, like my son, are now gone. The flowers, like all grieving parents' children, are gone. We took care of them, we nourished them, we guided them to grow, but now they are gone, and we grieve.

We must now face winter. It is cold, dark and barren. As many of our hearts are. Nothing grows, the days are short, the nights are long, almost unbearable. For we must now face the winter of our lives without our children. And, as with winter, we have no idea how cold it will be, or how long it will last.

For us, all of us, this winter will be cold and long. And like grief, we can't get around it, we can't climb over it or go under it—we have to face it and deal with it. We will each deal with winter in a different way, as we do with our grief. Some of us hide and cry, and keep interactions to a minimum—we feel we must grieve alone. For others, we reach out, we ask why, we go to support groups. We need to hear from others that we will be okay one day. Some of us start foundations. We need to feel we can prevent other parents from suffering the loss we have suffered. We will all do something—and even if we do nothing, that is still our way of doing something.

We all deal with our own winters in our own way. That is what we need to do. But we will all make it through winter, as we will make it through our grief. One day we will smile again. One day we will plant again and see flowers. One day we will see spring and we will know we made it through this winter, we know we will survive our grief. How long or how cold will winter be? How dark and how long will the nights be? We don't know, no one knows. But we will make it through, we will see spring one day.

The very last picture of Andrew. He was truly happy in Boulder, and fit in there so well.

HOW LONG CAN I GRIEVE?
September 28, 2014

IT HAS BEEN a year now. A year since we lost our dear Andrew. A year since our dreams of watching our son grow into a man, watching him get a job, get married, have children, were cut short. In a tragic second, we went from proud parents of a son about to embark on his senior year in college, to grieving forever for  our son. We went from a happy life of enjoying music, food, and friends, to spending much of our time crying and talking to each other about Andrew and our love for him.

It has been a year. The longest and hardest year of our lives. We have had some terrible days, and some not so bad days. But never a good day. We now enter our second year, which we hear is harder than the first. And then our third, and fourth, and fifth, and on and on. It will never end for us. The grieving, the crying, the missing. We will live with it for the rest of our lives. The form our grieving takes might change. We might change. But we will be grieving in our way.

Some people have asked us if we are okay now. It's been a year, it has to get easier they say. Pam tells a story about the fact that she is five or six years out, and although her grieving has evolved and has changed, she is still grieving. Her friends find it hard to accept that she is still hurting, still grieving after all these years. The fact is her son is still gone—he is still not with her physically. She still lights candles for him, still talks to him, now more than ever. And probably will forever. But her friends can't understand—how can they?

The fact is we, too, will grieve for a long time, probably our entire lives. When we go to a wedding, of course we will be happy for the bride and groom and for our friends. But we will also cry knowing that Andrew will never get married. He will never have the joy of walking down the aisle and saying, *I do,* and being introduced as Mr. & Mrs. Andrew Grosser—and that hurts. When our friends have grandchildren, we will share in their joy. We will smile with them and hold their grandchild and be happy for them. And again, we will cry. We will

cry for the fact that Andrew will never know the pure love of raising a baby and watching that baby grow up. He will never stand there proudly as his son reaches his Bar Mitzvah, reads from the Torah, and becomes a man.

For all these things, and more, we will be there for our friends, and we hope and expect that they will be here for us. But our grieving will not end, we will not, and cannot, get over it. We are on a path that very few travel. It is a path of sadness, sorrow, and loneliness. But we will be on that path the rest of our lives.

When a parent is lost, it is the proper order of life. We grieve for our parents, we expect them to pass before us, and we eventually move on. We go back to work, we start to go out again, we have our children and our future. It is the normal cycle of life.

When we lose a spouse, it is harder. They are our present, they are our life partner. We know that one day one of us will pass before the other, and the one left to grieve will do just that—grieve. For a month, a year, a few years. But then again, they will move on. They may meet someone and fall in love again. They will go on with their lives and enjoy old age with someone, and sit on the porch someday not alone, but with someone new. We would want them to. They are not replacing their lost partner, for no one can do that, but they are moving on.

With the loss of a child, you lose your future. And you never get over that.

Some people are surprised that parents grieve for years and years. They expect us to get better, they expect us to move on with our lives. It's been two, five, ten years—and yet you still light candles and cry? You still visit the cemetery every week? You still invite people over for Andrew's birthday? Yes we do.

Just a few weeks ago we watched as the names of the victims on 9/11 were read, many of them still have parents alive and were someone's child. And we watched as their parents grieved and cried on live television, and it was okay. We understand their grief, and have compassion for them and their loss. It has been thirteen years and they still grieve, and people are all right with that, and the public grieves alongside them. Then why is it different for those of us who lost a child not on 9/11? Why are we expected to get over it sooner? Why are we questioned after a year or two or three?

I am of course not comparing our losses to those lost in that tragedy, but the fact is our children are gone as well. The parents of Sandy Hook children will grieve for the rest of their lives as well, as will the parents of the children taken in Norway. Although our children were lost in different ways, we all will grieve for the rest of our lives.

So, do we get over it ever? No. But we learn to deal with it. We learn to deal with the hole in our hearts, we learn to deal with the forever empty bed in our home. We learn to smile again, we learn to enjoy some things in life. We start to put our lives back together.

Some things will also make us cry. For me it is hearing any Beatles music. Andrew loved The Beatles, he understood and appreciated their music. Whenever I hear them, I am just overwhelmed. For Dorothy, it is a young man on a skateboard, for she always sees her Andrew on that skateboard, enjoying life.

So when you see us, any grieving parent, please understand that we are still grieving, and always will be. But our grieving takes different forms over time, it evolves, and we learn to deal with it differently. We might light candles, we might have a birthday cake every year, or keep our children's pictures all over our home. It is our way of connecting and never forgetting. It is our way of grieving. And to be honest—we don't ever really want to get over it.

JUST ONE DAY
October 13, 2014

DREAMS AND FANTASY—that is what helps us all get through the day. No matter how real or unrealistic they are, they help us survive.

The one dream I have, along with other grieving parents, is that one more day. That one more day that I can have Andrew back. I have no other dreams or wishes. Just one. Just to have him back for one day.

What would we do? I have given that so much thought. I have spent hours sitting in the chairs by his fire pit thinking about it, planning out the day, wondering what it would be like.

What comes to mind is to talk to him the entire day—that is if I could ever let go of the hug I would give him first. We would have breakfast—a frittata with eggs and potatoes—he loved to wake up to that in the morning. Although I have been making it for a while now, he still loves Grandma's the best. I am sure he would hug Daphne and Buzz. Every morning the first thing he did was to jump on my bed and roll around with the dog and the cat, hug them, shower them with praises, and make them feel so very loved.

After we eat, I am sure he would want to take a shower —a long, hot shower. He really relaxed in the shower and always said it gave him piece of mind. I still have his body soap in the shower, and I actually bought a couple more of them—Dove Men's Care Extra

Fresh. Once in a while when I shower I will use just a dab of it. Just that little dab makes the whole bathroom smell the way I remember Andrew. It brings back such a visceral memory of him—like he is standing there and I can still smell him. It hurts, but the memory is so clear and vivid.

We would sit outside by his fire pit, all four of us, and talk for hours. There is so much I wanted to tell him, but never got the chance. Of course he knew he was loved so much, but there is so much more. There are things you wait to tell your son as he grows up, everything in time. But we have no more time.

My father holding me and my sister, many years ago.

I told him a little about my dad, but not enough. I told him about how I grew up, and the difficult time I had without a father, but did I ever tell him that it worked out okay? I don't know, but maybe he knew that. What did he think of me as a father? I promised him I would take care of my health and do my best to be there for him and Nicole as long as I could during their lives. I never broke that promise.

And the things I have for him, I want to show them to him.

The things he was supposed to have one day. I have my father's war ribbons and decorations (he earned a Silver Star as well as two Purple Hearts) and his Eagle Scout patches—stuff that I am so proud of, that I wanted him to know about. But I wanted him to be a little older, a little more mature, before I shared them with him. Maybe after college. I wanted him to have my grandfather's cuff links—they are so beautiful. It was supposed to be his gift when he started his first job. Now they are still in my jewelry box, but I know what I am going to do with them at least. I have a baseball that was given to me by my team when I played little league so many years ago, which is signed by everyone on the team. It has been on my work bench getting worn all these years. I played for only one year, but I drove in the winning run one game, and they gave me the signed game ball. My father was so proud of me; I remember it to this day. That is something I would have wanted him to keep on his desk, or have on his night stand for him to remember me by one day when I was gone. I would spend some time showing him these things—knowing he can't take them with him, but that he would appreciate knowing about.

Hey, do you know how to set up an NAS (Network Attached Storage) box? Or do you know how to change anti-freeze or change the oil in your car? Can you help me fix this thing or that thing? Have you ever seen "2001: Space Odyssey," or "Animal House"? Wanna watch it with me today? These are all things that I have thought about since he is gone. All the things that I never got to say to him, show him, teach him. So many things, that I probably would need more than a day. But I would have such a need to show him so much stuff—just so he would know.

We would just sit there and talk. His mother Dorothy, sister Nicole, and I would just look at Andrew and feel so lucky to have these hours with him.

Andrew used to be upset that it took me too long to do some projects around the house, procrastinating until I eventually got to them. He would joke that maybe it would be done before he came home for the summer, or came home for spring break. Well I've gotten through the list of those projects, and I would want to show him that. I know he would smile. And I would share that I have learned not to procrastinate too much. That is something that always bothered him, and I promised him I would change it—and even now I am keeping my promise to my son.

We would leave him alone with Nicole for a while. He would want to hear about how she is doing in college. How difficult it was for her—her first day of school without him there to talk to. "How was your first year?," he would ask. How are your teachers and your classes? And most important—how is the food in school? He would tell her stories of his first years of college, and how sorry he is that he never got the chance to finish. He would be so proud of her playing college hockey, and wearing his number to honor him. Andrew was a person of few words, but I am sure he would tell her so much about college and how proud he is of her and what she has accomplished so far in her life.

There is so much more to the day that I imagine. But after I write all this, after I think about all of this, it would not really be like this. We would spend the day, the entire day, with Andrew snowboarding in Vail. That is what he loves, that is what set him free, emotionally. They might have beautiful mountains where he is now, but nothing like Vail. Why would I be so greedy as to deny him one more, one last day of snowboarding. There  is so much we need to tell him, need to show him, need to hold him. But he knows all that. We would just let him snowboard. And we would be there and watch him smile, try to keep up with him, and just let him enjoy his day, not ours. It would be his day.

And then we would sit there together as the sun goes down over the mountains. And, as he told Dorothy when he came to her in her sleep on Mother's Day, he would get up and say, "You know I have to go now."

KEEPING MY RELATIONSHIP WITH ANDREW ALIVE
October 11, 2014

WHAT DOES IT mean to have a relationship with someone? Does it mean talking to them on a consistent basis? Seeing them once in a while? Having fun together? Bouncing ideas off them? It means a lot of different things to different people, and it is almost impossible to really define. But as I see now, it takes  on a whole new definition; a whole new set of parameters.

I still have a relationship with my Andrew. I need to. It has evolved into something different, and is still evolving. It is very esoteric, very emotional, almost theoretical. But it is still my relation-ship with my son. And, as I have said before, I need to have this relationship if I am going to stay sane and emotionally stable for the next five, ten, or however many years I may have left.

It is very different from my relationship with Nicole. I see her every couple of weekends. I get to watch her play hockey and cheer for her. I get to hug her after games and tell her how proud of her I am. We go out to dinner, I take care of her fish, I get to help her wash and clean her car, and we text once in a while (probably more than we talk). I get to ask her how school is, I worry about her when she is hurting, and share in her joys when she is happy or excited about something in life.

With Nicole, we are still growing. The relationship we have is still developing and will continue to develop for our entire lives. I find joy in making her happy. I love to cook for her when she is home and eagerly await her feed-back about my attempts. She is coming home this weekend for a few days. I am making a frit-tata with caramelized tomatoes, spinach, potatoes, and onions for breakfast on Saturday and inviting  Grandma over. Saturday night I am grilling marinated flank steak, seasoned sliced baked potatoes, spinach, and some dumplings for an appetizer. I am making spinach pasta with fried pancetta one night, with grilled romaine lettuce and blue cheese salad. And we are making fresh sushi rolls together on Monday (spicy shrimp rolls, shrimp tempura rolls, salmon rolls, and more).

It's a lot of work, but it is more enjoyment than work. It gives us time together when we prepare and cook—time that I cherish. Deeply. The one comment that we will make a few times over the weekend—Andrew would have liked this. Or maybe he wouldn't have. But we will talk about him. We will keep our relationship with Andrew alive through our conversations about him. We use the soy sauce that he loved and which he picked out—he was very picky about his soy sauce and let us buy only one brand. Maybe we won't say anything about it, but we know we are using his soy sauce, and that would make him happy.

But back to Andrew. ...

I still talk to him. I still tell him how I feel, how I miss him, what I am feeling at that moment, that I still cannot believe he is gone. I sit in his room sometimes and look around and imagine him there. I remember the good times when he used to build with his Legos, and when he used to take apart his paintball guns and replace parts and rebuild them. I keep his closet clean, I refold his clothes for him once in a while, and rearrange things around his room so that I can see different things at different time. I have his Titans Hockey jacket hanging on his doorknob now so that I see it every time I walk down the hall. Before that it was his black-and-white-checked flannel shirt.

He is no longer physically here, he no longer tells me about life and what he is doing. But on many levels, I am much closer to him now than I ever was. I used to think about him a lot. I used to have him in my thoughts much of the time, as well as Nicole. But now he is constantly in my heart, he is constantly with me. My relationship with Andrew is still very give and take. I get so much comfort thinking about the wonderful, but much too short life he enjoyed. I get a smile on my face knowing that he loved life, he loved what he did, he loved to travel and snowboard and live in Boulder. He loved his friends, and he had such great relationships with his close friends that he enjoyed. The thoughts he gives me are cherished, and the memories he gave me for twenty-one years are what keep me going these days.

I started to scan the photographs we have from when Andrew and Nicole where born, to when we got digital cameras. There are hundreds of them, and I look at each one and smile as I set it down on the scanner. Each one of them brings back memories and builds my relationship with him.

Some can say that he is no longer here and can't give me anything going forward. I disagree. Just like a father whose children grow older, move away and start their own loves, who is left with the memories of them growing up, going to school, playing sports, and traveling. These are the same memories I have of my son. As I remember them through thought or pictures, they build that relationship with Andrew. And they keep that relationship alive for as long as I can remember him, in my thoughts and loving him in my mind.

As we get older, we forget things in life. We get new memories and forget the old ones. It is a natural cycle. That is why I have to keep my relationship with Andrew growing. I can't bear to lose a single thought of him. I can't bear to forget a single detail of what he did in life, and how he looked and how he smelled, and how he drove, and how he loved. This is why I write  about him. I need to be able to one day look back over these journals and pictures and make sure I never forget Andrew.

IS THERE EVER A BETTER TIME?
October 22, 2014

ANDREW WAS TWENTY-ONE. We had twenty-one amazing years with him. Julius was only two and a half. Lisa was thirty-four. But their losses are equally hard on us.

We had Andrew for only twenty-one years. Or should we say we had him for a full twenty-one years? We got to watch him grow up, to learn to walk and talk and go to school. We were able to be there with him to celebrate his Bar Mitzvah and to stand with him for his high school  ice hockey senior night. We watched him graduate from high school and get into his first-choice college. We even got to help him select his major and make it three-quarters of the way to completing it. We feel so blessed for the time we had him.

 But what did we miss? There are so many things. We missed to chance to see him graduate from college. We missed

him starting his first job and hearing about his first day at work. We missed joining him as he started a family, having children of his own to raise. And most of all we missed him growing to be a fine father and family man. And we missed so much more. But we did get to see so much.

Mark and Elaine had their wonderful daughter, Lisa, for thirty-four years. They got to experience many of the childhood and teenage events we had with Andrew, plus more. They were there to celebrate their daughter's graduation from law school. They saw Lisa grow into a successful attorney over the years, buy her own apartment in Manhattan, fill it with beautiful art, and make partner at her firm. These are things we will never see.

But does that make it harder or easier on them losing her? Are they more blessed than we were with the time we had Andrew? They got to see so much more than we did. They got to have their daughter for another twelve or so more years than we had our son. They experienced so much more. So  maybe it is harder—they became so much more attached over those years and grew to know her so much more. Or was it not so devastating? She had lived a lot longer, she experienced more, and she left them with so many more memories.

And then there is Julian. He passed at only two and a half years old of a brain hemorrhage. His parents were able to shower him with love and affection for only thirty-two months. Were they better off than us? Their time together was so much shorter. But they never got to hear Julian speak his first sentences or watch him learn to run and play. They never saw him make friends or have his first day in school. He never told them that he loved them—like Andrew told us so often. That must hurt them so much never to have heard these words. They nurtured him for two and a half years, only to have him taken away suddenly and with no warning.

And now they live with watching other children, Julian's friends and relatives, grow up all around them. They know in their minds that Julian would have started school this year—and they missed dropping him off for his first day. His friends are now speaking and talking in sentences and asking questions. They are running around and playing and growing, something that they will never experience with their son.

Is it harder on the grieving parent who had their child only a short time and never got to experience these milestones of their children's lives? They put so much time, patience, and love into the earlier years--to have nothing to show for it all of a sudden. Now they have to live their entire lives asking themselves what would it have been like if our beloved child was still here. Or is it easier on them because they never had the years to get attached to their child and to develop that relationship that takes years and years?

How about the child that passed at fifty of cancer? He leaves behind a loving wife and three young children. How hard is it on his parents? They had him for so many years, he has left behind a legacy of grandchildren that will continue to grow and love. Although he is not with us anymore, his family is, and that means so much.

Now for the reality? There really is no difference. No one suffers less, no one suffers more. How long we had our child makes no difference at all. The parent who lost their daughter after a year suffers just as much as the one whose love was for twenty-one years, or fifty years. The fact is, losing a child is a devastating loss. There are no words that can be spoken to a parent who lost a child to give them

It's not just us who lost Andrew. Everyone lost him.

comfort. The loss is so devastating, so indescribable, that there is not even a term to describe a parent who has lost a child—for any reason, at any age. It is something that just puts a parent into a place that cannot even be described.

Why did I write this then? Why, if it is so hypothetical, so speculative, to compare the losses? Because it is something that we talk about in our bereavement groups. It is something that other parents talk to us about, both bereaved and those lucky enough not to be. It is something that should be talked about and needs to be talked about.

There is a saying that we hear a lot in our new circles—it almost sums it up.

When you lose a parent, you lose your past.

When you lose a spouse, you lose your present.

But, when you lose a child, you lose your future.

I hope you understand this.

IS IT MY FAULT?
October 31, 2014

IS IT MY fault?

Did I do something wrong? Did I miss something? Could I have done something differently?

What could I have done to save my child? Where did I drop the ball? Where did I let my child down?

There are many stages of grief. Some people say there are eight, some say there are five, while others say there are eleven or so. But this is the one stage of grief that everyone has on their list. Some call it anger—anger that we didn't do  something we could have—or that the doctors didn't do something that we could have asked or pushed for. Some call it reflection—where we reflect on what happened and deal with it. While others call it self-blame. No matter what you call it, no matter where it lies on the list, no matter how much you don't want to face it, every bereaved parent does. It is a healthy and a required step to deal with, and resolve, in order to move on to the next stage of your grief.

Fault, blame, responsibility, maybe omission, accountability. Whatever you call it—was it my fault? That is the question that haunts so many of us.

A couple we are friends with lost their child when she fell down a flight of stairs after she had drunk too much. They were not there, she was in her twenties and lived alone. She came home from a wedding and while trying to open the door to her apartment, she lost her balance and fell backwards down the stairs. They blamed themselves for a long period of time. They were mad that they didn't drive her home that last night to make sure she got into bed. They were mad that they didn't teach her better not to drink so much, or to ask someone for help if she was in no condition to get home alone. But as off base as that is, as much as we all see that it was not their fault, they still had to reflect on what they could have done differently. In no way could they have foreseen this. No way could they have brought her up differently to prevent this tragic accident. But still, it took them time to get over it and realize that they were not to blame.

For many parents, especially those of young men who pass away from drug overdoses, it is particularly hard. They looked at their sons over several months or years and watched as they deteriorated. They saw what was going on, the drugs taking over their child's life. They helped them by sending them to rehab facilities, both locally and far away. They spent tens of thousands of dollars at the best places that were available. They helped their sons by bringing them to doctors who were so called "experts" on addiction. They educated themselves on addiction in order to help their boys. They stayed home with them when they needed it. They showered them with love and praise and gave them everything they could to help them get through the addiction.

And yet, they died. And yet, they still overdosed. They ran away from the facilities, they found the drugs they needed, they got back together with those who were such terrible influences on them. And they tragically died. Very young.

Those parents ask themselves every day—what could I have done differently? What more could I have done? Where did I fail my son? And they cry over it. Not only for their loss, but for the blame that they feel.

But they didn't fail. There was nothing more they could have done. They tried their best and their children knew it. They spent their money wisely, and they did their research. But addiction is a massive disease, and there are no rehab facilities that really work. Addiction is overwhelming and all-consuming. Some people, especially those with co-occurring disorders, just can't get over their addiction. The doctors and the therapists just don't work sometimes. It is hard for me to say, and hard for many to understand, but these young men were destined to pass away young. They were stricken not only with ADD, ADHD, OCD, but they also had very addictive personalities.

Their parents go through a long time of remorse and thinking of what else they could have done. And until they learn that they did everything they could have, it is hard for them to get over their grief and pain. No, it was not their fault. If their sons were here today, when they come to them in their dreams, when they come through a psychic, they all say, It wasn't your fault--you did everything you could do.

Even for me, was it my fault? I look back and question myself. Three days before Andrew passed away he asked me for a new skateboard to go to and from classes with. His current one (of many) was getting old and slow. I of course wanted to make him happy, so we went out the next day and bought him one. It had great IBEK 7 gliding ball bearings built for speed, and wheels built for cornering and traction, and the board itself had great flex designed for control. But was it too much for him? Was the board beyond his abilities? If I had bought him a slower, cheaper board maybe he would not have fallen that day and broken his hand. And if he had not fallen and broken his hand he would not have taken the medications

the doctors prescribed. And if he would not have taken the medications, his lungs would not have shut down at night. And he would still be with us today. That thought process plays out in my head over and over again. And the doubt that I could have done something different is always there.

It has taken me a long time, but I realize it was not my fault. There was nothing that I could have done to stop what happened. If I had made him wear wrist guards, would that have helped? Maybe. Or a helmet? Maybe. But it was not to be. This is the way he was, this is the situation that happened, and what happened was a freak accident, and it cost my son his life. It changed so many other lives as well. But it was no one's fault. It was not his fault, nor was it mine. And that has taken me a long, long time to realize.

A friend's son passed away recently of complications from cystic fibrosis. She is going through the blame process now, and I feel for her. She was there to protect her son. She was there in the hospital to make sure he got the best medical treatment possible. She did all that. She fought for him, she guarded him, she held his hand. She did everything right—and yet he is gone. She is left with dealing with his loss and the blame game.

Unfortunately he was stricken with a debilitating and deadly disease. She loved him. He was a successful person in life because of her. He taught Yoga and Philosophy—which she should be proud of. In her thoughts, did she do enough to protect and save him? It will take her weeks, or months, or years. One day she will come to peace with her answer. She will be at ease, realizing that she did everything right. He passed away because of a disease—not because she missed something, or for something she could have done. She has to realize this one day in order to move on in life, in order to properly grieve, in order to smile one day. She will always cry for her loss, she will always cry for her son, but the tears will be of memories, not of fault.

We all have to realize this one day. As I said, for some it takes months, for others it takes years. And for some, the unfortunate few, it never happens.

Even for the parents of a child who passed away from a brain hemorrhage in just a few short hours—could they have gotten him to the hospital faster, or could they have recognized he was tired sooner? It was not their fault.

Or the parents whose child was kidnapped and murdered. Did they not teach her to be safer? Did they not give her the tools to properly protect herself? Did they not teach their son not to race his car? Where did they fail? Where did they mess up?

Or the child that passed away in a ski accident, or playing hockey, or from anorexia/bulimia. It was no one's fault. It just happened.

Is it their fault? No. No. No. Easier said than accepted. Easier listened to than learned. It is one of those stages of grief that many grieving parents get stuck in—sometimes forever. But it is one that we all must face, one that we all must look into the deepest recesses of our minds and deal with. We have to realize that we did protect our children the best we knew how. We did everything we could have done to protect them, to love them, and to shelter them. But somehow they passed away. Somehow they got cheated out of the rest of their lives. And in order for us, those whom they left behind, not to get cheated out of the rest of our lives, not to cheat the family that they left behind, we must face this question and answer it. Answer it only to ourselves. And then move on to loving our missing children forever, knowing that they are still loving us and will be there forever loving us.

"You cannot save someone—you can only love them"
—anonymous

For more information on co-occurring disorders—please see the Harris Project: https://www.facebook.com/theharrisprojectCOD

REGRETS OF WHAT ANDREW MISSED OUT ON …
November 7, 2014

I AM SITTING here on my flight from New York to Phoenix in row 7, just a few rows behind that infamous opaque curtain that covers the elite first class. I gaze up there where they get to eat Caesar salad, herb steak, and cheesecake for lunch, while I munch on the chicken I took from home and a bag of grapes I am traveling with. I don't mind it. I have been upgraded to first class a few times, and while it was enjoyable, I don't miss it.

What does come to mind is a regret. I see the people up there smiling, sitting comfortably in their wide seats, and getting pampered by stewardesses that are actually nice. It bothers me that Andrew will never have that experience. It bothers me that my son will never have the chance to be one of those who are pampered in first class. I know he would have enjoyed it.

What else has he been cheated out of? What else do I think about that he never got to do or see? Where didn't he get to go? What did he forever miss?

He never got to Israel or Italy—and I know he wanted to go to those places. I know he wanted to go with Todd and Jeff to Israel —he talked to Jeff often about going with him one day. He wanted to see what so many people had so much faith in. He talked about going to Italy with Dorothy and Nicole—he wanted to see Bonefro, where Grandma is from, and share in her memories of her times there. He never got to go to either place.

He loved snowboarding. He went every chance he had when he was at school. He went to Vail more times in three years than most skiers go in a lifetime. He snowboarded every mountain there as well as the back bowl—where only the most skilled boarders dare to go. He loved Vail, and I got to experience it with him many times as well—these are some of my best memories with him in the recent years—especially the times Nicole went with us. When we were there he talked about going boarding in the summer up in Canada. He talked about going boarding in Italy and the Alps, maybe being dropped at the top of a mountain from a helicopter. Again, these are things he never got to experience—he only got to dream about them. And those dreams are gone now.

As we all know, he loved to drive. He loved to drive his Jetta and absolutely loved to drive his six-speed RX-8. Windows down, sunroof open, stereo wailing away, wearing his cool Ray-Bans and his ski cap. He would have Eminem or some rap artist playing, but not too loud—he liked to hear the motor running and the sound the tires made against the pavement. Thanks to one of my closest friends, Andrew also got to experience driving an amazing Porsche. What a smile he had and exhilaration he felt. In that instant, he knew he wanted one. He could feel that was in his future. All of a sudden, he had a goal he wanted to achieve. We also talked about going to driving school in Connecticut together, where they teach performance driving—emergency handling, high speed turns, handling spin-outs, learning how to corner better and to really take advantage of what his Mazda could do. But once again, he was cheated. We both were.

We were also supposed to play in an adult hockey league his last summer. But his broken hand prevented that. It took away our father and son time—it cheated us both. Luckily we did play in a few games together the prior summer, and I will cherish those memories. Andrew said I was too slow on the ice, and I couldn't shoot—like I needed my son to tell me that. He said if I stood in front of the net, he would pass me the puck so I could score. I am not sure if that worked or not, but at least he tried. I see so many other dads from my adult league play-ing hockey with their kids, and I know that I am being cheated

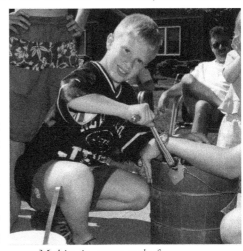

Making ice cream at the farm

out of that. I see the pictures of them together on Facebook, huge proud smiles on their faces. And I will miss that. Maybe Nicole will let me play on her team one day.

I look in his room at what he did have. Bracelets he made at

the farm in New Hampshire where we spent time as a fam-ily every June. Wrist bands from the cruises we took. An armrest from his high school auditorium. Some broken hockey sticks, tro-phies too many to count, and I smile at those things. I smile at what is there, what he left behind of his experiences.

I know he loved our visits to East Hill Farm in New Hampshire every summer. He had such good farm friends that meant so much to him. He kept everything he ever made at the farm to remind him of the good time. This past summer, our farm friends made Dorothy and me a scrapbook of pictures of Andrew, and notes from those who knew him at the farm. It means so much to us to have that scrapbook. We know how long it must have taken them to make it, and we appreciate it, we look at it all the time.

He loved to spend time with his friends in town, by the woods, or in a parking lot nearby. Just hanging out. He would sit out there with the same people for hours and hours and talk about the same stuff over and over again—all the while with no shoes on. I guess the no shoes were an Andrew and Wally thing.

I see his paintball markers (guns). He had pods, and masks, and bags, and all the other accessories that he needed to play for hours. Back in high school, he and a bunch of his friends would go to Park Lane, where there were dozens of unexplored acres and they would play all day. They would break for lunch and Grandma was always glad to make something for him and his friends, or we would have pizza brought in, then back to the paint.

Some of our closest friends with us on a cruise
Photo courtesy of the Image Group

He also has the ticket board I wrote about before. How many kids his age get to experience The Who in concert—not once but twice. We all got to see an unforgettable evening with Meatloaf in the front of a very small venue. He went to numerous Jets games, Rangers games, playoff games, World Series, NBA Finals, and so on. He was a certified SCUBA diver at thirteen and we dove all over the Caribbean—together—especially with his sister and mother.

There are so many things to smile at in his room. I have to learn, as have so many others, to treasure what he did get to see and do, to treasure what he treasured, and to know he had a great life.

So I look up in first class, and I know he never got to experience this. But what he did experience was amazing. What Dorothy and I were able to give him during his lifetime makes us happy. Now I can close my eyes, take my nap, and know that for the few short years that I had him, I gave him whatever I could.

CAUSES, PASSIONS, AND FOUNDATIONS
November 15, 2014

CAUSES, PASSIONS, AND Foundations. We all have charities, causes, benefits that we like to support. It makes us feel good. Whether it be a center for the arts, a public school foundation, a food bank, or drug prevention—most people support some cause to some degree. I think this is great. Some people put in a few hours a year to work at a fundraiser one day, while others work several hours weekly for their causes. Some people can raise hundreds of thousands of dollars just by making phone calls to their friends and business acquaintances, while others raise money ten dollars at a time for their charity. No matter what you do, no matter how much you raise, it is important to be involved with something that is meaningful to you—for it is your emotional attachment to that cause—this is your motivation. It is not your friends or colleges asking you, not your moral obligation to do something—it is how that charity and cause has affected you that drives you do be involved on some level. It is an almost visceral reaction that causes your attachment to this cause.

Like many others, I have been involved with a few charities over the years. Attended meetings, helped at golf outings, raised some money, spread the word about a specific cause, etc. But was I passionate about any of these? Not really. I guess that is why I was involved with them for a few years, and then moved on. Like most of us do. Our kids outgrow soccer, so we stop being on the board. Our kids graduate from high school, so we move off the educational foundation. We get a new job, and we change our charities to be in line with our new company. But we move on because there was no emotional attachment to the cause.

Unfortunately, it is the traumatic and horrible experiences of our lives that force us to change and re-evaluate this.

A friend of mine was the victim of a roadside bomb in Iraq and suffered a traumatic brain injury. He has fully recovered, thankfully, and now runs a foundation for injured warriors—a foundation that has raised and invested over $20 million to benefit our warriors returning home. This is an amazing feat. I am sure he was involved with many other charities before the accident—but now he and his family are passionate about this cause. They were personally touched by it.

Another friend of ours, Stephanie, lost her son to a drug overdose. The family spent tens of thousands of dollars sending him to rehab facilities, sending him to the best doctors, and trying everything to help their little boy. Unfortunately, none of these facilities were prepared to deal with a teen with co-occurring disorders. This is where a person has a psychological disorder (ADD, ADHD, Addictive personality, etc.), as well as a drug dependency. Hence co-occurring issues. There is no real government position on this, the doctors are ill-equipped to properly help these children, and the medical/rehab facilities are at a total loss. Stephanie now spends countless hours every day and every week educating others, giving talks, raising money, and she even finds time to talk to other parents whose children are going through this, to give them advice and support. She is an amazing person who has found a cause that will help so many other families deal with this disease. She knows, and we all know, that what she is doing may prevent other families from facing the tragedy that she and her family have to deal with for the rest of their lives.

Tragically, Debbie's son was struck and killed by a New York City transit bus while he was standing on the curb waiting to cross the street. He was just standing and waiting when his life was cut short by a bus driver—one who should not even have been on the road. Since that horrific day, Debbie has been relentlessly working for New York City's Families for Safe Streets and was a major force in reducing the New York City speed limit to a safer 25 miles per hour. Her volunteer work with Safer Streets will save many mothers, fathers, families from receiving that terrible phone call that she and her husband received a few years ago. I am sure her work is not yet done. Although the speed limit has been reduced, there is so much more to do, and so much more that I am sure Debbie will do, to prevent the senseless deaths caused by motorists each and every day.

For Dorothy, Nicole, and me, we are not trying to save someone's life, or help our returning warriors, or make people drive safer. There are so many other people who have undertaken these worthy causes. We have a different passion, that's all--a passion that Andrew started many years ago. We are trying to help underprivileged children. We are trying to positively change their lives and help them be part of the team—whatever team that is for them. We are trying to make sure that kids who want to play sports are given that opportunity. For those kids who want to play a sport but cannot afford the equipment or the special clothes or the cost of a mouth guard, we want to make sure they can still participate. We don't want to see children not play soccer because they cannot afford sneakers, or not play hockey or other sports because their stick is broken, or they lack a baseball glove or lacrosse stick.

So many grieving parents that I see have taken up a cause. Many other people who have been profoundly affected by some tragedy have taken up a cause. And these causes are all worthy.

But why does it take this grief to make someone want to help others so much? Of course there are people who work just as hard at their cause who have not lost someone, or who have not been profoundly affected. They do it because they love it and they want to do it.

Nicole's first high school's motto is "Not for Self, but for Service." Nothing about learning, or making money, or getting ahead in life—but service to others. I think that is great.

The point of this entry? Get involved. Find something that you want to do. Don't sit back and let the opportunity to help others pass you by. Talk to your friends and ask them what they do. Find something that makes you tear up or that you can make a connection to. Help at a food bank (on a day other than Thanksgiving), walk dogs at a local shelter, help socialize stray cats for a cat rescue group, collect coats for the homeless, help set up computers or build homes for returning vets. But do something. Get out of your chair and step up to life. Don't rely on others to do it.

Had someone not been passionate about breast cancer and started to raise money for research, do you think the survival rate from breast cancer would be in the nineties? Had someone not been so passionate about not throwing away food every night, would City Harvest save some 136,000 pounds of food each and every day? There are dozens of other examples of people getting involved to help others.

Don't sit on the sidelines and let the opportunity to get that feeling of helping others pass you by. Sit up, take responsibility, get involved: it will change your life.

ALL OF A SUDDEN
November 25, 2014

A LOT OF what I write about is what I hear and what we discuss in our bereavement groups. I take in so much in these groups, I churn it, I digest it, think about it, and, when I can, I let it out and write about it. Sometimes I use the person's name who talked about it; other times, I just write about what so many people mention.

In tonight's meeting, Pam talked about a drive to go shopping on Route 84. She passed a pretty bad accident—ambulances, airlift helicopter, police cars, and mangled vehicles. But what caught her eye and her mind was the covered dead body on  the side of the road. Obviously, someone did not survive the accident. She could not see if the person was a teenager, or a senior, or someone's son or daughter, or mother or father. She didn't know if the person was a reckless speeder who caused the accident, an innocent victim that was just driving along and had his/her life ended, or merely a passenger in the wrong car at the wrong time. She knew nothing—but there lay a dead body.

What we all thought—and Pam verbalized it so well—was that in a few minutes someone's life was about to change. Someone, maybe parents, maybe a wife or a husband, maybe a son or a daughter, was about to get a devastating phone call that would forever change their life. This person lying under the blanket on the cold blacktop could have been someone's only daughter, or someone's father, or a husband. And the person or people left behind were going to get a call in a few minutes that would be the worst call they will ever get.

"Hello, this is Sgt. Smith from the Connecticut State Police, can I please talk to ..." And that's it.

Right now, that person can be playing tennis, or working in his office, or at school, or on vacation somewhere having an amazing trip. They are living day-by-day, very happy with their life. But that will all end very soon. With just one call, their life's path will forever be altered.

Most people who see this scene look at the body and feel sorry for that person who is dead. They probably died too young. He or she was such a wonderful person with so much to live for; they were taken from this world way too early. There are so many thoughts for that person. But they are gone. They feel no pain now. They have no grief. They are somewhere else, wherever that may be. But they are no more—they will not cry for those they left behind, they will not grieve for leaving this earth. Wherever they were going, they will not get there, whatever they were doing will never be completed. All of a sudden, they are gone.

But those they left behind: As grieving parents, most of us have received that call. We may have been at work, or at home in the middle of the night, or on our cell phones. We have received that call. The call from some unfortunate person forced to give us the news that our child is gone. Gone forever from our lives. Each and every one of us can tell you exactly what we were doing before that call. What we had planned for that day, plans that never got completed. We were happy, we were watching TV; we were enjoying ourselves and feeling lucky to have such great lives. We were just going merrily along looking forward to so much. Then we got that call.

As grieving parents, yes we are sorry and feel for the person lying on the side of the road, bloody, covered, forever gone. But we feel for his or her parents, we connect with them. We feel for his or her wife or husband. We feel for the children left behind. We feel for that phone call. We relate to them so much more, we empathize with them—we are them. We are the ones  who received that call that changed our lives, the call that devastated the happiness within our hearts. The call that forever changed the life path we were on.

All of a sudden.

PROMISES AND MISTAKES
December 8, 2014

I JUST LEFT a small software conference and heard something very refreshing. The CEO/President and the Chairman of the company that convened the conference opened the conference up with a pretty typical state-of-the company speech. What was refreshing about it was that during their opening remarks they said that over the past year they had made some mistakes, they had made some misjudgments, they had stated anticipated changes and made decisions that had not come to fruition. All of the consultants there knew that already, but it was refreshing for them to say that, and to own it, it gave us a respectful perspective. We quickly moved on, now that it was dealt with, and the entire conference was very positive and successful.

I lay down that night and thought about Andrew, like I do every night. I had made him promises and told him what I was going to do during his life. Told him how I was going to raise him and protect him. Promised him the sun and the moon. Of course he was only a few days old, and probably didn't understand much of what I said, but I still made him promises. And to make it worse, I reiterated these promises throughout his life.

To stand by him and to support him throughout his life, no matter what he did, no matter how he turned out. Now I am here, alone, staring at the darkened ceiling knowing that we never fulfilled these promises. Some of them he was too young for us to fulfill. Others we just never did. While many others we did fulfill in the short time we had him.

The other part was a little harder to face. Mistakes.

Andrew, I made mistakes during your life. Some of them caused you pain, some of them made you cry, others just made me cry. Some of them were obvious, while others were visible only in hindsight. But I definitely made mistakes. All parents make mistakes, we are not perfect, and raising a child is an on-the-job learning experience. We learn as we do, and as you grow. Maybe we learned a little too slowly, or a little too late.

But most parents have a lifetime to correct their mistakes. Or at least to make right by them. They talk to their children, they discuss what happened, and they move on. Their mistakes become learning experiences and help  them as their kids grow up. Your mom and I don't have that chance—and it sucks.

Most of the mistakes are small. Insignificant in the course of a lifetime. I always drove fast—and you learned by watching me from the back seat, which probably explains why you got, let's say, more than one speeding ticket. I am sorry that I didn't slow down and set a better example for you. I know I upset you when I argued with someone over insignificant things, like a bad hotel room or a price discrepancy—and I tried not to when I was around you—but I did it way too often. I know it's too late to teach you better, but you will be glad to know that I really don't do that much anymore. You have taught me to be much more compassionate, patient, and understanding. Unfortunately, too late for you to appreciate it. But I know that you know that you have changed me for the better.

In the grand scheme of your short life, I know that these  broken promises and mistakes are minor. I know you had a great life, I know that you know you were loved and cared for and your mom and I did our best to raise you—and we are doing our best to raise Nicole. I know these mistakes were immensely outweighed and outnumbered by your positive experiences, and I am at peace with this. I can close my eyes and recall the good memories. But I wanted you to know that I am truly sorry for these mistakes. One day, somehow, I hope that you can let me know you forgive me.

All parents make promises that get broken. All parents make mistakes. But it is those of us who can put them into perspective and make them relative who can properly love our children and grieve for them unconditionally. We cannot dwell on the promises we broke, the mistakes we made, the unspoken apologies—for they are in the past. We must remember our children, remember the good, remember the love, and hold on to that as we move one foot in front of the next.

TO KNOW, OR NOT TO KNOW
December 19, 2014

Nothing more beautiful than snow on the mountains in Colorado.

SEVERAL YEARS AGO, a good friend of mine, Robert, had a terrible brain tumor. He knew what was happening in the beginning, he knew what he had and what was wrong with him. But, with time, he lost much of his short-term memory and, eventually, middle-term memory. As long as he knew you from years past, he recognized you. When Roy and I went to visit him in the hospital, he knew us. But when Andrew joined us, Robert did not know or recognize him, although he had been there visiting him just a few weeks before. Robert slowly declined as the tumor grew, and he really did not question why he was in the hospital, or what was wrong with him. He could hold a conversation with you, and talk about life, and he always seemed happy. He didn't know how sick he was, and never questioned the tests or the radiation treatments. He eventually went home, and he passed away in the shower a few months later—never knowing what was going on with his health. Never knowing that he was so close to death for so long.

Was he lucky? I don't know. He was dying for well over a year, and he was never sad. He never cried about it, he never thought about what he was going to miss out on in life. He didn't cry over not getting married, or having kids, or traveling the world. He was just happy all the time, all the way to the end. He had no idea he was ill, no idea his days were severely limited. He was just living his life.

Is this better than knowing?

Another lifelong friend of mine, Karen, also had a brain tumor that slowly took her life over the course of several years. But she knew it from the very beginning. She looked into the eyes of her two young girls and knew that she would never see them grow into lovely young women. She knew that she would never see them graduate from high school, go off to college, and one day get married. When I visited her, we talked about life and the past. She was bedridden for months as her body slowly deteriorated over time, and she cried. She talked to her mom and to her sister and friends to make sure that her daughters were taken care of. She was so concerned for their well-being, and she wanted to make sure they had a great life—even without her in it. She wanted to make sure they went apple picking and visited Disney World. She wanted them to know all about her. My friend Dee and I saw her a couple of days before she passed, and we talked all night with her. She knew the end was so near, she faded in and out of consciousness but wanted to tie up so many loose ends with so many people. Her body was getting frailer by the day, but she brought out that smile and laugh every time her daughters were there.

I can only imagine what she went through those last months. What would anyone go through knowing that they are going to die soon? We all know we are going to die, and it is a part of life. But we don't know when, and we all hope it is far, far away. We don't prepare for it mentally, we don't prepare for it spiritually, and we don't talk about it. It just happens one day, for most of us.

But those of us who know they are going to leave us soon, either from cancer, or a tumor, or whatever terrible cause, what do they do? It is terrible that they are going to die, but is it a blessing that they have time? They can talk to those they love and tell them everything they want to. They can tell them stories of the past, they can tell them things they never did before. In some cases, they can make peace with relatives long forgotten, and bring family back into their lives. They have time to make things right, they have time. Maybe a few days or weeks or months, but they have time to repair the past, they have time to make amends.

Or is it a curse, knowing that your days are so numbered? Knowing you will not live your life out, you won't grow old. Living with the stress that every day you wake up you are that much closer to the end. Going for the tests and hearing the dreaded results day after day, week after week. Watching your body as the disease slowly kills you.

Some parents who have enough time have made video-tapes for their kids to listen to. Some have written long journals to leave behind. They know they are leaving and they want to be remembered, so they do whatever they can to leave something meaningful behind. They want to leave some sort of legacy, some proof they were here on this earth and made a difference.

But as I said before—how can they mentally handle knowing that they are dying? It must be such a burden, such an unnatural thought, something that our brains were never designed for. People can relate really only to something they know, and this is something that not many of us can really comprehend—knowing our days are so limited and so finite.

Andrew was in the first group—he never knew. He never knew he was going to die so young. He never knew he would not make it to graduate from college, or get married and have a family. He didn't know how finite his days were. He made himself sushi for dinner, he watched TV, called to say goodnight to Dorothy and me, and then he just went to sleep. That was it. He passed very quietly and peacefully in the middle of the night, not knowing what he had missed out in life. Not knowing anything.

He never let me know what to do with his car, or what to do with his snowboard—who should get it. He left his valuables just lying around in his room. His phone was charging, his computer was left on, his laptop was downloading music and videos. He had no reason to think he would not be with us in the morning. It was to be his first day of class, he had bought all his books, he got his notebook ready, he even wrote in his calendar, "First Day of Classes." He didn't know.

As I look back on this, and as I learn more about grief and suffering and pain, I am almost thankful for the way he passed—not that he passed, but the manner in which he was taken from us. Andrew was a fragile soul. He was a kind, gentle human being. He thought things out in such detail, and always questioned everything, in a positive way. He had compassion for anyone and everyone he

met. He had no hate, no fear, no animosity in his life. He was happy every day—but he did not handle stress well. He loved everyone he knew, and always helped others. He had no enemies. His coaches always told us that no one ever disliked Andrew, His teachers welcomed him into their closed classrooms for lunch, just to sit and eat and listen to him talk about life. He loved to listen to others as well.

There is just something so peaceful about this picture of Andrew.

I know he never had the chance to say goodbye. He never got the chance to tell us things I am sure he was holding inside. But I am okay with that.

He never had to look into our eyes and say goodbye to his mother, his sister, and me. He never had to tell us those things that bothered him. He never had to hold his beloved pets and say goodbye to them, knowing he would never see them again. That would have hurt me so much more. The pain that would have caused him would have been so much, I would not have been able to bear it. And I do not think he would have been able to handle that either.

So the question is—is it better to know and have the ability to make peace, but live with the knowledge the end is near? Or is it better to just lie down and pass—oblivious to the fact that your life as we know it is about to end?

So tell me—are you thankful for the way your close ones passed? Are you at peace with the way they were taken? Or would you have liked it some other way? Of course we would all have liked it not to happen, that is a given. But it did happen to us, and we are left here to think about it for the rest of our lives.

THE SECOND YEAR
January 2, 2015

"YOU'VE MADE IT through the first year, the worst is over."

Every grieving parent has heard that, numerous times. Whether it be from a friend, family member, colleague, client, or customer, we all have heard it, Dorothy and I included. It might be worded a bit differently, might be said at different times, but we all have heard it all several times. When it has been said to us, we have smiled, we have been courteous, said thank you, finished the conversation, turned and walked away. We know the person saying it has such good intentions and means it to help us, but where they draw this idea from we don't know—and we hope they never do know our pain. We listen to what they say, make eye contact, and smile at them, but inside we cry a little more. Inside we hurt a little more. Inside we know that is the furthest thing from the truth.

Last year during Thanksgiving, we sat at the table without Andrew. It was the first holiday for which he usually came home from college. It was his senior year and all of his friends came home to their families. Nicole came home. And yet—no Andrew. We had our turkey dinner, we had desert, we talked a little, but there was nothing to be thankful for. Our Andrew was not with us. It was the first holiday without him, the first of many. We were realizing that this was our new reality.

Then it was Hanukkah and, soon after, my birthday. Both very empty. Then Dorothy's birthday, Christmas, and his twenty-second birthday, and New Year's Eve, and Nicole's birthday. He was not here to celebrate any of them with us. We tried to make these special days as normal as possible, we tried to be with family and friends as much as we could. We tried to celebrate in ways that we could. But it hurt. It was always the first time.

It was the first Christmas tree at Grandma's house without Andrew putting on his favorite ornaments. It was the first year Dorothy and I went holiday shopping for one child, not two. It was the first birthday in so many years that my son did not call me to wish me a happy birthday. There were no gifts for Andrew anywhere. There were no cards for him, no calls, no nothing. And it was the first time. Everything was different. Everything was hard. But we made it through that season of firsts.

There were other firsts and events as well. It was the first Mother's Day on which my loving wife's only son did not call her. We sat at the Passover table for the first time and he did not participate in the four questions—for the first time. We went on a small vacation over the summer, for the first time, just the three of us.

Everything we did, everything we saw, everything in that first year was a first. And it was so hard to get through them. The first this, the first that. Every time anything happened, or we did something together, we realized that Andrew was not there with us this year. We realized that we were alone, the three of us.

People tell us that we made it through. Of course we did. We had no choice. We had to keep our feet moving, our lives had to go on. We still had to work, Nicole still had to go to school. We placed his headstone at the end of that first year with many of our friends, Andrew's friends, and family by our side. The first year was over.

Then in September the second year started. And people told us that we had made it through the toughest times of our lives, and many said it would get better. Even though they never experienced what we are going through, and it is to be hoped that they never will, they reassured us that things get better. They never experienced their child's birthday—AFTER their child was gone. We very much appreciate people talking to us, calling and visiting us, going out to lunch or dinner with us, and helping us. Without our great friends and family that we are grateful for, that first year would have been so much more difficult. We are very grateful for the special people in our lives. Without the conversations we have had with them, the healing conversations, the stories we share, the sympathy that they show us, we don't know what we would have done this first year.

That first year taught us one thing—over and over again. That Andrew was gone, that he was no longer with us. We cried a lot, just about every day. We looked at pictures of Andrew every day; they are all over the house, our computers, and our phones. The shock wore off after the first few months. Then the pain set in. The realization that he is gone cut deeper every day.

But now we are in our second year. And it is worse, but in a different was. Here's why: Through the High Holidays, Thanksgiving, birthdays, Hanukkah, and so forth, Andrew is STILL not here. We know that. But we now have to face the cold fact that he will never be with us again. Ever. He is gone ... forever. He will never help us carve the Thanksgiving turkey or smile when he opens his Hanukkah gifts. He will never have dinner with Uncle Roy, or go skiing with Todd and Greg. He will never again help decorate or see a Christmas tree. He is gone forever. In year three, and four, and five, and for the rest of our lives, he is gone. And that hurts more than the first year when he was just not here. We went from the deep pain that he is not here to the searing realization that he will never, ever, be here again.

Yes, the first year was difficult—missing Andrew at every holiday, birthday, and family gathering. But the second year is harder. We now have to face the reality that he will never again be with us for the rest of our lives. And that hurts.

I could not find any places in this post to appropriately put pictures of Andrew and the family, but I think the pictures I post are an important part of each post. So here they are at the end of the post. All showing how happy Andrew was all the time.

Photo courtesy of the Image Group (left)

Apple picking—lots of fun

Showing surprise and awe at Bubby's 65th.

MEETINGS
January 15, 2015

IT HAS BEEN sixteen months since we began this terrible, tragic journey, and almost every week, like clockwork, Dorothy and I go to our bereavement group meetings.

We belong to a few groups. They are all over the calendar. One meets every other Wednesday, one meets the second and fourth Tuesday, and one meets the first Thursday. On average, we go to one meeting a week, two some weeks, and no meetings other weeks, but over the months, it all works out. Each group is very different and there is almost no overlap among members. The locations are all different--one meets around a dark brown conference room table, one in a cluster of comfy seats and couches in a church library, and one meets in a church meeting room dominated by generic 3' x 6' tables. One group charges a few bucks per person per meeting, while another serves us free pizza at every meeting. One is run by a professional therapist, the others by trained group leaders. One is part of a national network of bereavement groups that holds national and local events, one is run by a local bereavement center, and one is affiliated with a local hospital. All of them so very different.

But the meetings all have one thing in common: they are gatherings of parents—and, in a few cases, siblings—of lost children. We come together to talk about and honor our children, to talk about everything that is going on in our lives, to support others who have recently joined the group, and to come to a "safe" place. What we talk about and what we say in the group stays in the group. We sometimes share photographs of our children—we want the others to see what our beautiful son or daughter looked like. We share songs they might have written, or poems that we found that help us and might help the others, or mementos that meant a lot to someone. But we mainly talk. This is a gathering of our special group of people. These are the people who "get it." Even though they think they do, or as hard as they try, no one else really does.

Sometimes there is a topic that we talk about. In November and December we talked about the holidays, how they are without our children and what we do to honor our children who are not with us anymore during the holidays. In the Spring we talk about new life, new beginnings, Easter and Passover: and how they relate to what we are going through. In June, we talk about graduations: that some of our children never made, or that their friends graduated and what it means to us that our children did not walk down the aisle that year. Sometimes we talk about what we constantly are doing to honor our children and keep our relationship with them alive. Sometimes we just start and can talk non-stop for ninety minutes; other times the leader has to keep us moving forward, because we all are frozen in our thoughts and pain.

If new parents come to the group for the first time, something we all know too much about, we listen patiently as they talk about their loss. Sometimes it is too raw for them to share, too soon for them to open up, and they say just a few words, tear up, cry, and they tell us to move on. We understand where they are at, we all have been there. We see them over the weeks and months come out of their painful shell, come out of their shock. Eventually they tell us about their son or daughter. Sometimes they can't use the word *died,* or *passed,* or *lost.* The first time a parent says that in front of a group is a huge realization for them. We all know why they are here, and we all know that they lost the most precious thing a parent can ever have, but the first time they say it out loud, even in a whisper, is a milestone for all of us. To this day, all I can say is that I lost Andrew. I can't describe it any other way. It's just too hard to say any other words.

Some families and parents come to the groups for years–once, maybe twice a month. Their children died five, seven, ten, or more years ago. They find peace and comfort in coming to the meetings. It is a safe place where they can go and talk about their child. They can cry openly and not be judged, they can show pictures and tell stories to people who are genuinely interested. They are never asked if they are over it yet, or whether they have moved on. They are around people who actually know what they are going through, unfortunately. They are around their peers. They are with the other members of a club that no one wants to be in but that we are forced to be in by circumstances.

There are those who, like us, have been going for a much shorter time, maybe a year or two. We are still learning to deal with our loss. We look forward to going to the meetings, for it is our safe place, as well. We can openly cry there—we are actually expected to cry at the meetings, as most of us do at one point or another. We regularly see a few other families who lost their sons about the same time we lost Andrew. We went through the holidays for the first time together. We went through the process of picking out a headstone together, and so much more–but we went through them together with people who understood. We had people whom we could lean on over the year who were going through the exact same thing we were, and it helped us so much. We were there for them, and they were there for us.

Some people come to the group once or twice. The can tell their story, they can listen to what we have to say, but they do not return. Talking about it, or listening to others, just hurts them too much. They have to deal with their loss in a different way. We don't know why they don't return, they just drop out, and they are gone. But we hope that they are, in their own way, dealing with their loss and their grief. We intend to stay, for now. For another year?

Two years? Five? Neither of us really knows. Do we want to be going every week in five or ten years? I don't think so, neither does Dorothy. Will we be cured, will we be better, will we be over it? Absolutely not. But we hope to one day be at a point where we know how to deal with our loss and out pain, where we can talk about it and not cry so much, where we can help others through the pain.

We were helped by some of those parents who have been in the groups for years. A few months ago, Pam, who lost her son several years ago, gave Dorothy a little piece of paper with something written on it—simply, "It will get better, I promise." Dorothy was having a very tough time and this little piece of paper, these simple words from someone who had gone through the feelings and pain Dorothy was feeling now, helped her so much. Maybe one day we can help someone else in this same simple way.

He always had a smile on his face.

Andrew and Mom

They enjoyed playing together all the time. He looked out for Nicole and made sure she was safe all the time.

MOVING
January 22, 2015

MOVING. WHAT A broad subject. Not moving on, or moving up, or moving others with your words. Just moving. Packing up everything you own, everything your family owns, your pets, your possessions, packing it all into a truck, and moving. Shutting down and leaving the home that you have known for so long and going to a new start. We all do it a few times in our lives, some more than others, others only once or twice. Sometimes we move for work, or for a larger place, or for downsizing. But where I am now, my mental and emotional place in life, moving has different meanings. Moving becomes emotional.

Every day, every *single* day, I visit Andrew's room. It might be for just a moment, to touch something, smile, and leave. Or it might be for a few minutes to look at his belongings, do some remembering, and then get back to my day. But every single day I go into his room—I am with him for that moment. Sometimes when I am lost, I sit on his bed and ask

Andrew's shelves: his snowboarding glasses, his many hats and sunglasses, pictures of Daisy, the manual to his car, Jovi's birthday gift, and so much more of him.

him for advice. I think about what he would say to me, think about what his thoughts might be. I might just think about him, about his smile, about what his life could have been. It gives me great peace and comfort to have that place I can visit. His room. His stuff. His memories. It is such a large part of my moving ahead with my life.

Sometimes it is sad for me to go there, sadness beyond belief and something that no one can ever put into words. But those days  are getting fewer and further apart as I learn to deal with this loss. But they are still there once in a while. The days that I go in there and smile and recall the good times, recall the blessing that I had with my son for twenty-one years are becoming more frequent. I look at his guitar and think about the joy and pride he had learning to play it. It still sits on his bed where he left it. I look at his high school yearbooks and read what his friends wrote to him, and I smile. I look at his team jackets and how honored he was to wear them and be part of the teams that he was on.

Then there are the things that only those who knew Andrew would appreciate. There is an armrest from the high school auditorium. Why would someone want that? Who knows, but Andrew had it—and was proud that he had it. There are his pads of late passes and hall passes from high school. I don't know, but I am sure his friends know why he had them. And his sneakers—for someone who never wore shoes, he had a lot of them.

When I go in there, I connect with him. Many of his clothes are still where he left them—although cleaned, folded, and put away. Some of his books, *His Ranger and Titans Jerseys, his hoodies and jeans. This is what we remember him in.*

some of what he collected, some of him, is still there. And I need that, I need to know that and see that to get me through each day and to keep my feet moving forward. I cannot see that day in the future where I can box it up, store it away, pack up what is left of Andrew and move away. Maybe one day it will happen, but maybe it won't.

But for others it is different. And I understand that. For others, the site of their children's room, seeing their empty space, seeing the toys that lay collecting dust, the clothes that will never be worn again, the books that will never be read, is just too much. The searing pain of their loss is brought back to them every time they pass that doorway. Sometimes the door is kept shut, so they do not have to see inside the bedroom. Other families keep the door open, and bear the sight of the room. Their loss is tied to that place, tied to that house, which used to be a home. For those parents, a new beginning, a new place, a fresh start, is what they need. They need new surroundings not tied to the past. Simply put—a move.

They have to put their son's or daughter's belongings away. They have to box up the memories, box up the clothes, the toys, the books, and prepare to move. They might sell the furniture, or donate it, or pass it along. But it does not go with them. It is too hard to keep it. They are downsizing, they are relocating, they are moving to a new place where the memories of raising their wonderful child do not exist.

One day they will open those boxes again and sort through what was their loved one. They might cry over a toy, a book, or a piece of clothing. But it is not an entire room of overwhelming memories. It is not the entire home where they spent so many loving years before that fateful terrible day. These tears might be of the happy times, the happy memories. These tears are the good ones that moved along with them.

Don't be mistaken—when they moved, they took their children with them. The memories, their love, all that was their child, all that they had, moved along with them, but they are moving. We never forget our children. No matter where we go, or where we stay, what we give away or what we choose to keep, our sons and daughters are always with us. But some of us have to move away and start over, while others chose to stay.

Why the difference? Why the irresistible driving force to stay put or move away? Just like all grief, just like we each handle our grief our own way—no one knows why, it just is.

This journal is written in honor of Emily, and in memory of Daniel, as a thank you for all of the parents that she has helped move ahead in their lives and all of the souls she has healed.

AS TIME GOES ON, YOU FORGET US ...
February 3, 2015

I WAS AT the funeral of a friend and client of mine several months ago; he passed in his mid-fifties, suddenly and unexpectedly. During the eulogies, one of his siblings spoke about his wife and their love for each other. He spoke about the family and the friends that Ray had during his lifetime and how much they meant to him, and how close they were. This was pretty much expected. Then he went off on a tangent and spoke of something unexpected.

After telling us how much Ray's friends and family meant to him, and all that they had done together, he asked us, all of us, not to forget his wife—his widow that he left behind. He said that of course we will all be there for her in the upcoming days and weeks and months. But as time goes on, we will move on, forget about contacting her, and make other friends. He asked that we each take a personal vow to stay in touch with her, to take her to lunch some time, to not forget about the friendship in the upcoming year, or two or five. Everyone in the room, everyone at the funeral, was an important part of their life and he implored us not to forget her as time goes on. As a widow whose children are grown and moved out of the house, with their own lives, she is all alone now. All she has is her friends—us—and we had to be there for her.

We all agreed and we all understood.

"I don't hear from my friends anymore."

"My friends are not comfortable around me anymore."

"I don't have anyone to go out to lunch with."

I hear that all the time in my bereavement groups. It's not just from those who lost children. It's from widows and widowers. Children who lost their parents. And people who lost a close friend.

I saw it firsthand when my father passed away when I was sixteen. My parents had a lot of close friends. They went out every weekend with friends. They belonged to groups and clubs. They were very active. But that all stopped when my mom lost her life-partner. Yes, of course, some of her friends stayed in her life, and they are there now. But most of them disappeared over a rather short period of time from her life. She made new friends, she met new people, and she moved on. But I know it hurt her, and it hurt us, the absence of the so-called friends who disappeared soon after sitting Shiva. This is an all too common scenario.

I know it is hard to stay in touch with someone whom you no longer have much in common with. Or someone with whom it hurts for you to have lunch because of the memories. Or the dear friend's spouse with whom you were never really close to begin with. Or an in-law, once the bonds of the family no longer exist. I have been there as well.

But think of it from the other side. Ray's wife is now alone. She can use the occasional phone call or e-mail. She could use the occasional lunch or dinner date. She could use the shoulder to cry on, or the friend to recall the happier times. She needs friends—her old friends.

The same is true for the bereaved parent. You don't know how much it means to us to receive a text or an email that just asks us how we are doing. The short phone call to say you're thinking about us, or that Andrew was on your mind. It doesn't take long, and it means so much. Now I am not writing this for ourselves. Dorothy, Nicole, and I have a lot of friends and family who keep in touch with us—and we really appreciate it so much. It has helped us get through this whole tragedy and kept us talking about Andrew and kept us alive. Dorothy still goes out with her cousins every few months, and she needs and appreciates that. They are as much a part of her life now as they were before. It's not about us. It is about so many others that we know, so many others that we speak to and hear from, so many others that don't have that tight network of family and friends that we do.

We know parents who have lost their only child, and their friends just disappeared from their life. Fortunately, we do keep in touch with several of Andrew's friends, so I know how great that feels. We know husbands who have passed and their office mates just moved on. While others stay in the widow's life and help her to move on.

We have been to a few funerals in the past year or so, too many, really. We hear all the time from the visitors that they are going to stay in touch, that they will call, that if the grieving need anything, they should reach out to the visitors. Well it doesn't work that way. They are not going to reach out to you. They are not going to call you and ask you to take them out to lunch. They are not going to send you an email and say that they are doing okay, or that they really need someone to talk to. It just isn't the way it works. They are the ones with the loss, it is way too hard for them to reach out.

It's up to you to reach out to them. Let me say that again. It is up to you to reach out to them.

I am sure that most of us have been to a funeral a year or two ago of someone we cared for. Someone who meant a lot to us. Maybe, as in Ray's case, someone who was a friend and a mentor to me. Or someone who lost a parent they were close with? Did you tell them you would be in touch? Did you let them know you were there for them? Did you promise to be their friend? And then, did you turn around and walk away and leave them?

I'm just saying …

Do you think it is time to reach back out to them? Do you think he/she deserves that helping hand and that soft shoulder? I know that the initial call would be hard to make after all this time. But how hard is it on your friend not to receive that call? Not to be consoled and to not feel forgotten. It's harder on them to be left alone, and it hurts much more, than it would be for you to swallow your pride, pick up the phone, send an e-mail, send a text, and make someone feel loved and comforted.

Andrew was very proud of his little sister's preschool graduation. He was, and still is, very proud of everything she accomplishes in her life. He was so proud when she got accepted to play college hockey. He, sadly, never got to see her dreams realized, though.

Nicole and Greg on my roof. The backstory: We went apple picking, and to make it easier, but probably not that safe, all of the kids got to stand on the roof of my car as we drove from tree to tree to make it easier to get to the apples. No one was seriously injured so we had a very fun day.

Dorothy, Nicole, and Andrew at a Yankees game. Although he didn't enjoy the game, he loved to spend time with Mommy and Nicole. Much happier times for everyone.

I really don't know. Maybe he is doing some Vulcan mind thing on her? Or some Pokémon mind game?

LIFE STARTED OVER
February 18, 2015

NEW YEAR'S DAY, a new, insignificant, but much-touted starting point of time for most. Everyone changes calendars, starts their annual spending accounts over, hangs out with their families, and the new year begins. We all measure time: for good or bad, we do. We all measure our lives based on some random (or maybe scientific) timeline that started thousands of years ago. We have days, weeks, months, years—and for some, decades. In the beginning, we use hours and days, we move on to months and years at some point, and then decades as we approach some point in our lives.

Ask someone how old they are, that measurement from the day they were born until their last birthday, and everyone knows it. How long have you been married? How long have you worked there? How long ago did you graduate? And everyone knows the answers to these questions. They all know so many dates, and how long it's been. Everyone measures their lives against some, or several, events. For the most part, against happy points on that long line of life.

But with us, as with many others, it is different.

As Cynthia said a few weeks ago, life started over when she lost her son. It is the only important day, the only date that really matters anymore. There are plenty of other dates, but this one changed everything. Everything is measured from that day on—and will be from now on, for the rest of her life, as well as for the rest of our lives.

Our timeline has a new starting point now. We no longer measure how old we are or how long we have been married—time frames that we were so proud of before. When we graduated from school or how long we have worked at our current job just don't have that sense of importance anymore. We keep track really of only one important date—when we lost our child. Everything is still measured, time keeps moving on, but we just don't seem to care about those dates anymore. There is really only one date now.

Ask any bereaved parent, "How long has it been?" Before you can even finish the sentence they have blurted out sixteen months, or three years, or seven years, or six weeks. We don't have to think about it, we don't have to calculate it, it is just there, all the time, on the tips of our tongues and in the forefront of our minds.

It is such a tragic day, such a tragic thing that has happened, that nothing else is as important to us—life started over on that day. Something that we loved beyond belief, someone that came from us, someone who was part of our being—was taken away.

For those of us who are lucky enough to have one or two or even three other children, or blessed with several grandchildren, we of course know their birthdays, and their special dates. But, more importantly, we know exactly how old they were when we lost our child. You could hear us say "Jack was fifteen when he lost his brother, he is now, uh—twenty-one." We know how old they were, but have to think about how old they are now.

Life also started over because we are such different people than we were before. Such a drastic change in our lives, such a shift in who we have become, this warrants a new start date. The path that we are on now, the path that fate has put us on, has a mile marker 0 where our new journey began. Every day, every week, every year, we go further down that path, but we are never far from that mile marker 0. It is always fresh in our minds and in our hearts, and never further than a teardrop away.

Yes, we go on. Yes, we get older. Yes, we remember all the good times before that date, and cherish them. But for us, especially us, our lives started over when someone was taken from us.

I NEVER KNEW HOW GOOD LIFE WAS
March 3, 2015

Look how happy they both are in this picture. It makes me smile....

"I NEVER KNEW how good life was." I hear that from Dorothy every so often, as well as others. I never really knew what I had was so good—compared to not having it. I had my home, my two children, Dorothy had a great job she enjoyed, and my business was growing every year. We went on vacations; I enjoyed listening to music and cooking for my family, and looked forward to speaking to my kids and hearing what they were up to every so often. Life was good. I looked forward to a future watching my son and my daughter growing up, maturing, falling in love, and having children. Retiring one day and sitting at home, looking back on my life and smiling, and looking forward to a house full of grandchildren for the holidays. I had a lot one day. Did I appreciate it? I probably did, but maybe not enough. I hugged my children and my wife whenever I could. I told them I loved them. I smiled when I looked at their pictures in my office, I was thankful my life path was in a good direction. I was happy. All until I received that call late at night from Boulder. We get up in the morning, and there is food in our refrigerator, and clean clothes in our drawers. We go outside in the morning and start our car, and take that car to work or shopping or to go see someone. We take for granted all these things—our food, our clothes, our car. But the day when the car is not working we get upset and angry for not having it—without really appreciating the days that we do have it. When the television breaks or cable is out and we have no TV that night we are upset because we have nothing to watch, but, again, do we appreciate the hundreds and hundreds of days when our TV did turn on with the push of a button?

Such gorgeous and genuine smiles.

What I have learned through this is that I appreciate my daughter so much more now. I appreciate every second I spend with Nicole, every meal we eat together, every phone call and every text I get from her. I smile when I look at the pictures of her on my desk and browse through the pictures of her on my phone. I look at the pictures of her growing up—and I am glad that I was there for so much of what she did. I appreciate the fact that I was able to coach her for so many years, that I went to every concert and play she was in while at school, and that I went to every parent-teacher conference and heard her teachers praising her (most of the time). I appreciate it so much more--just thinking about it makes my eyes tear up. I appreciate it when she is home and we sit on the couch and watch a Rangers game. We don't have to talk, but just sitting there with her makes me happy and fulfilled. When she is home for the summer and watches baseball with

Dorothy, it makes her so happy. I don't particularly enjoy watching the games, but the time that I get to sit there with her, watching her, being proud of her, is time that I will never get back, and I don't want to miss out on it. When I go to her games and see her dressed in her college jersey, it makes me proud that she has worked so hard for so many years to reach that level of hockey—we must have done something right when we raised her. I have always appreciated these times, but the appreciation is so much deeper now and so much more emotional. I also have learned to appreciate what my father gave me so many years ago, what he taught me, what he said to me, the legacy that is my father. Although my time with my father was short, far too short for a young boy to appreciate, I have learned to cherish that time and really appreciate it. But I see others who do not appear to appreciate what they have. They take their lives for granted, they take their money for granted, and they treat what they have as if they can't lose it. I look at them and say to myself, please appreciate it. Please. Especially—please appreciate your kids— please appreciate your parents. One day you might receive that call that they suddenly are no longer with you.

I do hope that you never receive the call that we did one night. I would hope that no one would ever receive such a devastating, life-changing call. But I also hope that you appreciate what you have, whatever that is. Look at your children and smile. Take every breath and memory in, and realize that they are limited in number. Do you have another ten memories with those you love, or another ten thousand? Who knows? Will they say that you appreciated life and lived it to its fullest, or will there be regrets and sorrow when you are gone? Will you think of all the things that you should have said to your children, or to your parents or spouse, when they are no longer here? Or will you be at peace when the time comes? We all generally have good lives, some better than others. We smile, we play, we work, we travel, but do we really appreciate how good our lives are? I see friends who don't have a relationship with their children, and I have players I have coached who don't really talk to their parents, sometimes because of disagreements over minor or stupid things. Then they are gone one day and it is too late. After a game last year, I talked to one of Andrew's teammates/friends who had moved pretty far away. I asked him about his dad and he said he really doesn't talk to him much, they don't get along. We talked a little about it, and I told him what I would give to have a relationship with my son at this point in my life, and the fact that I will never be able to have that relationship again. A few months later I see he posted new pictures of him and his father on Facebook, shaking hands and hugging. Now, I don't presume that my conversation with him precipitated this, but I smiled and was happy about it. I was happy that they were talking again. I was happy that they learned to appreciate each other—and leave the crap aside. Think about what you have now, not just your material possessions, but also your family. Look at your spouse, your family, and your friends. Look at your home, your job, the things that you collect and enjoy … Now, close your eyes (after you finish reading this). Think about the unimaginable. Think about life without them, without any one thing. So appreciate what you have. And for your family and friends—let them know you appreciate them. As Dorothy says so often now— "I really never knew how good my life was before." P.S.—I have a few close friends review and edit what I write prior to my posting the entries. They make sure the post makes sense, they look for spelling mistakes, and check grammar. After reading and editing this one, my editor, and one of my closest friends since second grade, sent me this note—I really do appreciate it: "I hope you realize this philosophy of yours was not a result of Andrew's passing. That you believed and lived this all along and that Andrew was the beneficiary of it. I remember well and often recall when I was working my ass off and doing well financially, and you reminded me in pretty strong terms about what is important …"

DEAD PEOPLE
ARE ALL SO AMAZING
March 19, 2015

I CAN'T BE the only one to notice this. Or am I just the first person to write about it, or have the chutzpah to talk about it?

Every person I have talked to recently about someone who has passed makes that person out to be a saint, a mensch, a pillar of society. They were all wonderful people. They never said a bad word about anyone, everyone loved them, they always wanted to help others—they were one of my closest friends. They gave so much of themselves, they were always there for me, their family always came first, they were always there to help anyone in need. They volunteered,  they coached, they mentored. They were so successful in business and gave so much back to the community and everyone around them. Holy crap, they were amazing people.

Now I am not mean, or cruel, or unsympathetic—but, really? And the more tragic the death, the more amazing they were. I have never been to a funeral or a wake or visited a house of shiva where they talked badly about the deceased. Yes, it is common courtesy not to badmouth the dead, but why does it have to be at the funeral home or the cemetery that this starts—this is my point.

I hear people talk about other people. They talk about their being cheap—they never pick up the check when we go out for lunch or dinner, they never put on a fair tip for the waitress, they never pay their fair share. But as soon as they are dead they were the most generous, giving person around.

They talk about how they pushed their children too hard, they shouted at soccer and hockey games, even got thrown out of a few games. They berated the coaches and the refs as well as the opposing players. They criticized the teachers and the principal about how inept they were. But as soon as they die, they were the most supportive caring parents who were always there to support their children and their teams. They were always ready to run the carpool and support the school.

They talk about how they work late all the time, and work on the weekends. They don't spend enough time at home, they don't go to school plays or teacher meetings. They go on long business trips and spend too much time at the club with friends and not at home. But as soon as they die, their families meant everything to them and they could not give their spouse or children enough love, nor spend enough time with them, or take them on enough vacations.

For children—they talk about how they don't listen to their parents, they have a tattoo or for goodness sake a piercing. How wild they are, what poor athletes they are and how they should not be on the "A" team. They drink, they smoke, they cut classes and drive fast. But when the unimaginable happens, and their young child passes, they become the most compassionate and loving child, they were so funny and understanding. Everyone loved them and they had so many friends. Their teachers and coaches loved them. They talked to us for hours and were so in tune with what they wanted in life.

I could go on, but you get my drift.

Now, there is a certain compassion that we all have when someone passes away, and I don't want to disparage anyone who has passed away. But my point it this—why does someone have to die for us to see the good person that they are? Why do we first see the bad and the negative, the dark side of people, when they are alive, and then, all of a sudden, they are dead and they become saints? Do we have to talk about people as though we were on "Real Housewives" all the time?

We are all guilty of it, I have just become so much more aware of it from being in bereavement groups now. Every child or sibling we talk about is almost perfect. That is why, to some degree, I enjoy these groups. They are negative in terms of why we are there, but we talk of anyone in mostly positive terms. We very rarely, if ever, speak ill of our children, or of others. They were all wonderful, cheer-
ful, amazingly smart and loved individuals. Now, I know Andrew was all of these things and more. But he was also short-tempered sometimes, he drove too fast, was a little reckless occasionally, and, once in a while, left the house without saying goodbye. He and I fought about some stupid things here and there, he hung up on me once in a while (never on his mom, though), and was not really good with time management or showing respect for some people whom he felt did not deserve respect. You would already know these things if you really knew him, or talked to me about him before we lost him.

So once again, what's my point? Now that we talk about our lost ones in my bereavement groups, and I talk to so many other bereaved parents, spouses, and siblings, I have learned to talk positively about everyone. I don't think about their dark sides, nor do I seek them out. I don't talk about what was bad or negative, or what I perceive as a person's faults. I try to find something nice to say, I ask about what they were like, I look for the light and the sunshine—not the darkness.

Everyone has faults and a dark side—but wouldn't it be nice if we didn't talk about that so much, and more about the positive and what that person contributes to our lives as well as others?

And let's face it, how do we want others to talk about us?

I WANT TO KEEP YOU IN MY LIFE
April 10, 2015

ANDREW, MY BELOVED son, I want to keep you in my life. But more accurately, I need to keep you in my life. I want to get up every day and know you are still here. I want to be able to tell you things, and show you things, and to share with you. When you were here, you, along with Nicole, brought the light into my days and into my life. It is that light that made me get up every morning, look forward to every day, and made me smile. I want to keep that light alive, and keep that light burning for the rest of my life, no matter how long that will be.

When I see something that I know you would have appreciated, I want to know that you see it as well. I need to know that you can still see what I see and that it brings a smile to your face. You don't know how many times I see a beautiful or customized RX8, your last car, and think, for a brief split second, that I should take a picture to show it to you. Then reality comes back. Sometimes I still take the picture just because I know that you would have appreciated it. But I want to know that you see that car along with me. That you still appreciate a nicely thought out, customized, clean car. When Nicole makes a great save, or wins a difficult game, you don't know how many times I have reached for my phone to call you to share it with you, only to remember that you saw it already along with me. And I slowly take my hand off my phone.

When I see something sad or upsetting, I look around to make sure you don't see it, the way I used to when you were a child. But I know you have already seen it. I cannot protect you anymore the way I used to. You're an angel now, my angel, and you see so much more now. When something goes wrong, I instinctively try to protect you, but I know I am too late. I just hope that the things that made you sad when you were with us, the things that made you cry before no longer make you sad or cry. I know that you are here with us all the time, but it kills me that I cannot protect you any longer. I can't protect you from sad events, from mean people, from tragedy, from anything that a good father should protect his children from.

When I talk to you when I am alone and hurting during the day, do you hear me? When I sit outside by your garden and tell you about what is going on in my life, the way we used to talk, do you still hear me? When I look at your empty seat at the dinner table, do you hear my thoughts? I used to be able to look into your eyes and know you were listening. I used to be able to hear you tell me that you understood and appreciated what I do for you, that you liked me gently guiding you and appreciated my helping you to get through issues that we all have in life. Do you still have any of those issues? Is there anything I can possibly do for you now?

More important though—do you know I love you. More than ever.

Nicole is still here—and she is the light of my life now. I am so happy when we are with her, or when she comes home from school

to be with mommy and me. She has that bright, beautiful smile that just makes us so happy to see, and that laugh (or giggle) that just melts away anything else. She is doing so well in school, making great friends and playing and loving hockey. She is as confident in herself as any young lady and knows she can accomplish anything she sets her mind to. She tells me you come to visit her before games—just like you used to do. She wears some of your clothes, visits your room, and is making you a part of her life like she always has. When she made the ECAC hockey conference All-Academic Team, I know you were as proud of her as we were—and I am sure that, for a split second, she reached for her phone to call you and tell you, just like I did.

I am sure you will be with her and guide her for the rest of her life—for you are her one and only older brother. Giving her advice and guiding her in your own special way. Supporting her and watching out for her long after the rest of us are gone. I have to believe that. I know your love for her will never end, as hers for you will never end.

When it is a cloudy day, and gloomy both inside and out, one of those difficult to get through days for Dad, I look up to that cold sky in hope. Every once in a while I see a ray of light coming through, or a small piece of a rainbow—faint, small, fleeting. And I say thank you for looking out for me and letting me know you are still here.

And a little levity that I know Andrew would appreciate:

Andrew—Mom's credit card got stolen last week. But I am not reporting it yet.

Whoever has it is spending less than Mommy!

MY SON DID EXIST
May 7, 2015

MY SON DID Exist.

I have been noticing recently that assorted people do not talk about Andrew—I don't know if this is a recent thing, or just something I am becoming more aware of. I notice this at some dinners we have been at, or even over lunches. It is not at every meal that I expect him to be brought up in stories, I understand that. It is nice to talk about him, or have others talk about him.

Many times we are out with our closest friends or family and they will tell a story of my son. They will talk about him like he is still with us, recalling him fondly, recalling him with love. At times they tell us stories that we have heard a hundred times before, but it still brings a smile to our faces. The time Andrew cooked fish with Uncle Roy and had to shake them first as part of the ritual. Or when he would ask teachers questions that were impossible to answer. Or when Todd, Greg, Nicole, Andrew, and I went on our annual summer water park trips and how we managed to cut every single line—Andrew was not one for waiting on lines. I have heard these stories so many times, but I still love to hear them.

Andrew and Anastasia at Playland—always a fun place.

Once in a while we will also hear a new story, one that we never heard before, one that makes us laugh and teaches us a little bit more about Andrew. Matt tells us stories from the hockey locker room—some that we really can't share. Wally tells us about Andrew in school, or just hanging around town. The time they wore pizza boxes on their feet because they could not go into the restaurant without shoes. We are so happy to hear them—but what brings us joy is the fact that people are talking about Andrew with us, they are not forgetting him.

But all too often we do not hear about Andrew. We are with other couples or friends and they talk about their kids, what they are up to and about their college or sports. They talk about Nicole and hockey and Salve Regina U, her school. But they do not touch on Andrew. I am sorry to say, it feels to us like he never existed. It feels like he is forgotten and people have moved on.

Andrew was so proud of Nicole at her Bat Mitzvah

I talked about this to a couple of close friends and they thought of it in a different light. They thought of it as people not wanting to upset us. Or people just nervous about bringing up Andrew around his grieving parents. They are not forgetting him, but, in their eyes, they are protecting us from the pain. Trust me, the pain is there whether you talk about him or not. Being silent does not ease the pain; it does not lessen it, or make it go away. It only hurts more. We want to talk about our son. The son we will never see again, the son we will never hold again. We want to keep him in our lives, in our stories, in our hearts. Don't be afraid to bring up something that you think we are trying to get over or be are afraid to remind us that our Andrew is gone. We know this. Even through tears it brings us pleasure to talk about all our children, including Andrew. You do not need to walk on eggshells around us.

We know you want to tell us about your children, and we want to hear about them. Don't be afraid to share your joys, your celebrations, your stories with us. We are here for that, and we want to listen. But in the same conversation, please let us all talk about Andrew, and let us share, too. Yes, we have no new stories; there is nothing new for us. We may have told you this story or that story before, but that is all we have right now.

And when we smile, as Pam expresses it so eloquently, it is not because we are over it, or that we are better, or that the old Perry is back. It is because we are happy to be with our friends, and happy to be talking about our son.

This goes for anyone who has passed—whether it is a child, a parent, a sibling, or cousin. Talk about them. Share your thoughts and your joys and sorrows with their family. That is what they want. Not just today, tomorrow, this week, or next month—but from now on. Keep them in your hearts, in your minds, and in your stories. That is what we want. More than hearing about your sympathy for us—we want to hear your joy when you talk about our lost ones.

Andrew, Nicole, and Keisha. Keisha was with us for ten years loving and raising our kids.

Epilogue—By coincidence, Dorothy and I went out for a burger after temple Friday night, to a place far enough away from home that we would most likely not run into friends. But as luck would have it, we did. We ran into a pair of hockey parents from Andrew's Mariners days--parents of someone he had as a teammate for several years, and with whom we had spent countless hours at rinks, restaurants, and hotels but from whom we had drifted apart as our kids went their separate ways.

It was sort of awkward at first. We had not seen them for several years, long before we lost Andrew. They got up and hugged us, and told us how sorry they were about Andrew. They said he was a good kid and that they were shocked, as was everyone. We talked about hockey and about Nicole, and about their kids. It was very nice.

But more important, that is what we needed. Instead of ignoring us, or just waiving hello, they got up, hugged us, and talked to us about Andrew. Yes, we cried. But it was a good cry. Someone talked about Andrew with us. Someone who did not need to, or have to, but wanted to. Someone who knew him, and still has him in their hearts.

Because he did exist—my son did exist, and he still does.

The Elephant in the Room (with liberties taken with the name)
By Terry Kettering

There's an elephant in the room.

It is large and squatting, so it is hard to get around it.

Yet we squeeze by with, "How are you?" and, "I'm fine," and a thousand other forms of trivial chatter.

We talk about the weather; we talk about work;

we talk about everything else—except the elephant in the room.

There's an elephant in the room. We all know it is there.

We are thinking about the elephant as we talk together.

It is constantly on our minds. For, you see, it is a very big elephant.

It has hurt us all, but we do not talk about the elephant in the room.

Oh, please, say his name.

Oh, please, say "Andrew" again.

Oh, please, let's talk about the elephant in the room.

For if we talk about his death, perhaps we can talk about his life.

Can I say, "Andrew" to you and not have you look away?

For if I cannot, then you are leaving me alone
in a room—with an elephant.

WHY DO I LOVE HOCKEY?
May 19, 2015

This is one of my favorite father-son pictures that we ever took together.

SOMEONE BROUGHT UP hockey to me this past week. They said that they recall that both Andrew and I loved hockey and it was a common bond we shared. It held us together and we enjoyed it together. Yes, we both loved hockey—but for very different reasons. The same is true for Nicole—she loves hockey as much as Andrew and I, but for a different reason.

Andrew loved the sport of hockey. He loved the feeling of skating, the freedom of being on skates and gliding along, the feel of the stick and playing the puck. He loved to check, take the puck

away, make a shot, and fight in front of the crease. He was immensely into just playing the game. But there was something deeper for him. He just lived to be on the team. He went around with the team, went out to meals, hung out at school, and constantly reiterated and lived what his coaches taught him—the team is your family—and will always be.

It was his teammates and coaches who called and e-mailed us right after we lost him. Those who could not make the funeral sent their parents. The team sent food and condolences for weeks afterwards. To this day I e-mail and Facebook message several of his teammates. They want to make sure we are doing okay, and they share what is going on in their lives, and how Andrew is so missed by them.

Andrew Grosser Hockey Captain

Hockey to Andrew was part of his life. He did not identify himself solely through hockey, but he did know that hockey and his hockey family was a large part of his life.

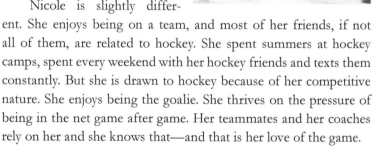

Nicole is slightly different. She enjoys being on a team, and most of her friends, if not all of them, are related to hockey. She spent summers at hockey camps, spent every weekend with her hockey friends and texts them constantly. But she is drawn to hockey because of her competitive nature. She enjoys being the goalie. She thrives on the pressure of being in the net game after game. Her teammates and her coaches rely on her and she knows that—and that is her love of the game.

She was at a tournament a few years ago and another team's goalies could not play due to illness. Their coach asked Nicole if she could play for their team (through Nicole's coach, of course). Even though this team was a competitor team for her, and her team would play them later on, Nicole was thrilled to be in the net for another game. It didn't really matter who she played for, but that she was in the net and that these strangers were relying on her to play her heart out. And she did—they won 3 to 1.

Another time when she was younger, probably ninth grade, a well-known prep school had two sick goalies—both out with SARS for a couple of week. After some finagling and approval by her school and the prep school league, Nicole was asked to fill in for this team as well. She was already playing for her school team that weekend, and for her travel team, but we managed to fit in two more games and an hour travel time each way—for two consecutive weekends. It was a very hectic time for us, but Nicole thrived. She played and played and played, but it was what she loves to do.

They both love the game, but as you can see, for very different reasons. Andrew loved being on a team, being part of a family, hugging his teammates after a goal, and being known as a Mariner or a Titan. Nicole loves the competition. She loves to make the stops, to stifle the competition, to play for any team that needs an advantage in the net. She loves to be known as the goalie—behind any jersey, but to be in the net.

And you then ask why do I love the game? Is it for the competition? Is it for being a Rink Rat for years? Or is it for the ten-plus years I coached and helped kids grow into great players? None of these, really—although I loved them all.

I love the game for what it gave to my children. I love the game for the thousands of hours, yes, thousands of hours, of quality time with Andrew and Nicole that it afforded me. Driving with them to and from over a thousand games, dozens and dozens of tournaments all over the northeast, or the hundreds and hundreds of

hours of practices where I had the chance to share the ice with them as their coach and mentor.

I can't recall how many trophies or medals we won as a team with either of them. But I remember the amazing feeling that I had hugging Nicole right on the ice after the state championship game where she delivered a shutout. Or the feeling I had when she won the Christopher Reeves Sportsmanship Trophy and I was standing next to her when she received it. Or the feeling when Andrew's team beat amazing odds and defeated teams that we were not supposed to beat—but we were a family, they were not. Or when Andrew's teammates voted him captain of the team and I was in the locker room to see his reaction. You can see in the pictures my smile—not for winning a piece of plastic, or for winning a medal, but for the joy and happiness the sport brought to my most precious children.

We have gone to tons of Rangers and Islander games. We have sat in sky boxes, press boxes, the owner box, and on the glass. Andrew had conversations with John Amirante before he sang; Nicole had lunches with Charles Wang and has been to closed Islander practices. They both have ridden the Zamboni, and have been to team parties. They have experienced so much happiness, so much in the way of thrills, smiles, and excitement, and have learned so much thanks to their involvement with hockey. And, again, we have spent so much good-quality happy family time together as a result of our family's ties to hockey.

That is why I love hockey. Not for what I took from the game, but what the sport gave to my children.

WHERE DO I FIND MY SON?
WHERE CAN I TALK TO HIM?
June 3, 2015

Sometimes it hurts to look at pictures,
to remember how happy we once were.

ANDREW AND I used to talk to each other often. Whether it be over the phone, via e-mail, texts, or whatever, we communicated a lot. I loved those father-son communications. They made me feel part of his life, made me feel that I was needed and that my advice was sought after by my son—something any father can appreciate.

That has all changed. The communication is now one way, and I am not sure if it is actually communication anymore. I talk to him, but does he listen? Does he know what I am saying? People are going to tell me he listens and he knows what I am saying, of course, but who really knows? I still have the need to talk to him, I still need to tell him what is going on in our lives and, most important, what I am feeling.

Where do I talk to him? Where do I go visit him? There are a few places.

One is in temple. That is probably the hardest place. It is in the sanctuary that I last gazed upon my son's beautiful face. It is where we had his funeral, where I last talked to him face to face. It is also where we had happy events: his pidyon haben when he was born and welcomed into the Jewish religion, his Bar Mitzvah when he became a man, and his Hebrew school graduation. It is where we went for his friends' Bar Mitzvahs, and for the High Holidays. We spent a good amount of time in that sanctuary—all of it happy until the very end.

I stop by the temple once in a while to sit there alone, in the dark, and gaze at the front of the room where his casket once sat. I talk to him. I tell him how I miss him, how we are doing as a family, and ask him how he is. Dorothy and I go together to temple Friday nights, but there are others there, and the mood  is much different. I look over at Dorothy once in a while and see a tear in her eye, and I know what she is seeing and what she is thinking—without saying a word. I enjoy going there; I recall things there that I cannot recall anywhere else.

I also visit him where his body now lies. He is not there spiritually, but his body is at peace at the cemetery. It is where I can see his name inscribed in granite: "Beloved Son, Brother, Grandson, Father." I am reminded of the cold truth that he will not see his son grow up, of how much his grandma and bubby miss him, and how much his sister's life has changed since he is gone. I also know that he is at peace there, alone but for a few other graves nearby, listening to the stream just a few feet from him, and that Daphne, sitting next to me, knows that something is special about that spot that we visit. I think it is only his body there, not his spirit, not who he was, but it is still nice to visit that small plot of grass that is forever his.

Where is he that I can talk to him? I think I connect to him most
in our backyard, in what is
now called Andrew's gar-
den. Andrew and I sat out
there many nights during
his last summer home, built
a small fire, and talked.
There is nothing out there
that was his, nothing with
his name on it, nothing
that he played with or held

Andrew's Garden

dear. But what is there is the memory of how close he and I were.
He told me all about his life, about how he learned so much from
the therapist he was seeing in New York to cope with his anxiety. He
told me how much he looked forward to his senior year in Boulder,
and how he was thrilled to be a psychology major now. We talked
about everything, including what I do for a living, how much I enjoy
my work, and what he wants to do for a living, and how he hoped
that he would enjoy his life's decisions as much as I do. He so much
wanted to help others and knew that one day he would. He asked
me about the cars I drove growing up, and how he loved to drive his
stick shift. There was no topic that was off the table. It was truly a
special summer talking to him by the fire for hours.

The one other place I talk to him is in his bedroom, which is
right next to my office, and pretty much the way he left it. Of course
we have cleaned it up a bit, and we have gifted or donated some of
his possessions to people who mean something to us, but it is still
the way he left it. We gave Andrew's desk and his suits that he wore
only once to Guillermo, who told me that whenever his grandson
wears them he thinks of Andrew and says a prayer. We gave Todd
his snowboard, so we know it is being used by someone who was
Andrew's closest confidant. We gave away little things here and
there so that the memory of Andrew lives on in other places, and
with other people. But there is so much more of him in the room.

I go in the room and sit on his bed. I smell his pillow, and I run my hand over his guitar. I look at the pictures of him, and at the things that he held close. I see his glasses that he loved to wear, his Rubik's Cubes, which he loved to solve, his hockey trophies, his team jackets, and his other toys. I sit there and I ask him how he is, where he is, and let him know how much

Andrew's guitar. He taught himself to play because he loved to create music.

we all miss him. I ask him why he is not here anymore, and that he really should be here. It kills me that he is gone, that my son is not with me anymore, that he will not grow up anymore—and I tell him that. But my pain falls on deaf ears.

The conversation is one-sided. I talk; that's it. Sometimes I look up when I talk and ask questions in the hope that he sees my face from above—and remembers me, and sees my love for him. Other times I hold my face in my hands to hide my streaming tears. It is different every time.

But I still talk to him, I still talk to my son, every single day.

FATHER'S DAY
June 17, 2015

I still do stand there next to you, you just cannot see me anymore, but I am still there.

HI DAD,

I have been thinking a long time of what I would write to you for Father's Day, what I want to tell you, as well as what you need to hear. And for Father's Day, a day that you have never embraced since the loss of your father so long ago, He has finally let me write you this letter. Of course it is your fingers doing the typing, but, by all measure, these are my words and thoughts—to you.

First of all, I know you miss me terribly, and we know you will never get over that. I miss you and Mommy and Nicole just as much. Just because we are separated, and I am here far away, I still miss being with my family—the family that I truly loved so much. But please take solace that one day we will all be together again, I know that. Hopefully not for a long, long time, but it will happen. That is the faith that you must have, that is what is going to keep you going. It will help you get out of bed every morning, and let you lie your head down on the pillow in peace at night. It will let you love

I miss the security and peace I found when I held you. There is nothing to ever replace that.

Nicole and show her the great loving life she deserves, and enable you to travel and vacation and see places around the world that you want to see.

As for where we will see each other again—that is a harder question. I know you have been told by some that I am in a "better" place—that is not entirely wrong, but it is not right either. I am in a "different" place. There is no real "better" place for me to be than by your side, with my family. But that said, I am at peace here. I have no stress, no anxiety, no pain. I feel that I am with many other people who came before me in our family, some I knew, some

We were always smiling and laughing when we were together. Please learn to smile again …

I have just met for the first time. The place I am in can't really be described—it just exists.

The peace they talk about is just that—peace. I do not have the joy of skating with my team, or snow boarding down a white snowy surface of a Colorado mountain. I cannot watch Nicole play hockey and cheer her on with the pride only an older brother can appreciate when his sister follows in his footsteps—even if those footsteps are empty now. I yearn to complete my life on earth, and not have had it taken from me.

I was sad, very sad, when you sold my car. That was my happy place, my comfort zone, and I loved that car. I know you had to sell it, it was the right thing to do, but it still hurt. I am happy, though, that it is now with someone who appreciates it as much as I did, and who is caring for it and loves to drive it as much as I did—but it is not me—it should be me. Peace does not replace that.

So on this day when I should be taking care of you, cooking you dinner, and thanking you for being the best father in the world, please know that I am at least thinking about you. Thinking about the great life you and Mom gave me and appreciating the time we did have together.

Now please, smile a little more, hug Nicole a little tighter, and enjoy Father's Day the best you can.

Your loving son, always,
Andrew

CONCLUDING THOUGHTS

I don't really like the section title Concluding Thoughts. It means that something is over, done, fini. This journey that I am on will never really be over. Losing Andrew, and living through it is rather a path that I am on for the rest of my life. What I make of that path is up to me. Likewise, what any bereaved parent makes of that path is up to them as well.

It is a conflict that we deal with. We mourn our lost children, but want to live our lives as well. We cry at night, but want to live the lives our children would have wanted for us. They are physically gone from us, but more present in our minds and thoughts than ever before.

Thank you for reading my story. Thank you for spending the time learning about Andrew, and listening to my struggles and dreams. Thank you to those who have not lost a child but wished to know what we are going through and how to help someone who has.

I hope that my words brought some peace and solace to your life. I hope that you can see some light at the end of the tunnel—or further down the path that we now walk. I hope that you now know that others have felt and experienced many of the same feelings you feel, and we are here to help each other.

And most of, I want you to know that you will survive. No matter how you feel today, or tomorrow, or next month—you will survive. And one day, eventually, you will smile again.

Perry

ABOUT THE AUTHOR

Perry Grosser lives in West Harrison, NY, with his wife, Dorothy, and their daughter, Nicole. He lost his son, Andrew in August 2013, at the age of 21. Soon afterwards, he started writing about his experiences, and how his friends and family interacted with him and how they saw the bereavement process—which is much different than reality. He has actively attended bereavement group meetings almost every week, as well as comforted many other bereaved families. Perry also spends his time with his therapy dog, Sam, visiting the elderly, and those recovering from strokes at a local facility, as well as visiting children with anxiety and sleeping disorders. This is Perry's first book but has plans to keep publishing and helping others in any way he can.

Visit the author's website:
www.NeverForgetAndrew.com

Connect with the author on Facebook

If you have any questions or comments, drop me a line:
Perry@NeverForgetAndrew.com

CPSIA information can be obtained
at www.ICGtesting.com
Printed in the USA
BVHW06s1944040618
518159BV00036B/1493/P